Something In The Air

Never content to rest on its laurels, Apple continues to push the boundaries of technology with the release of the iPad Air – lighter, slimmer and more powerful than ever!

There are two types of people in this world – those that love Apple products, and those that haven't used an Apple product yet. The iPad is yet another success story and it's a spectacular piece of hardware. Over 170 million iPads have been sold to date which is a truly remarkable figure, but not so surprising when you get your hands on one. The iPad Air is undoubtedly the most impressive iPad yet. It's narrower than its predecessor, the iPad 2, and more than a millimetre thinner as well. The slinkier casing doesn't mean any compromise in power or performance though. The iPad Air has all the grunt you could want.

If you've owned an iPad or other iOS device before then you'll know you way around it, although if this is your first foray into iOS 7 then things will look a little unfamiliar. We take a look at some of the major new features and improvements that have been made to the operating system starting on page 12.

If you're a complete beginner then this guide will get you up to speed on everything you need to know from the basic set-up process to using the iPad's more complex apps and functions. Our tutorials are broken down into simple steps so you can't go wrong. Once you've worked through them all, you'll be completely proficient with all your iPad Air's features and functionality.

For the gamers out there we've compiled a large and diverse games section, gathering together some of the best games in the App Store. We've also got lots more apps for you try out, some serious, some just downright fun.

Now then, let's find out more about this thing they call an iPad Air!

iPad Air

Contents

102 BOOKS AND EDUCATION

114 PHOTOGRAPHY AND VIDEO

140 ORGANISATION

150 COMMUNICATION

168 NAVIGATION

176 ACCESSORIES

Your iPad Air
And You

Welcome to your new iPad Air in all its glory. We've got a complete overview of this awesome device, its hardware and what makes it tick, along with an in-depth look at iOS 7. The latest version of Apple's mobile operating system is the most powerful and stylish yet and it's what underpins everything you do on your iPad.

Our anatomy feature explains what all the visible hardware features are, from the Home button to the Lightning Connector port, and we have an in-depth feature on iCloud. If you don't understand the concept of cloud storage, we explain exactly what it is and why you should be excited about it.

This section is really an introduction to the hardware and what it can do for you, so sit back, put your feet up and enjoy the ride.

"The latest version of Apple's mobile operating system is the most powerful and stylish yet and it's what underpins everything you do on your iPad"

Under The Hood Of The iPad Air

If you want to know what's so great about the iPad Air, check out these official specs, facts and figures. That wafer-thin case is crammed with the latest cutting edge technology.

169.5 mm (6.6 inches)

240 mm (9.4 inches)

Weight and Dimensions

Height:	240 mm (9.4 inches)
Width:	169.5 mm (6.6 inches)
Depth:	7.5 mm (0.29 inches)

Chips

• A7 chip with 64-bit architecture

• M7 motion coprocessor

Display

• Retina display
• 2048-by-1536 resolution at 264 pixels per inch

• 9.7-inch LED-backlit Multi-Touch display with IPS technology

• Fingerprint-resistant oleophobic coating

iSight Camera

• 5MP photos
• Autofocus
• Face detection

• Backside illumination
• Five-element lens
• Hybrid IR filter

• f/2.4 aperture
• HDR photos

Facetime Camera

• 1.2MP photos
• 1720p HD video

• FaceTime video calling over Wi-Fi or cellular
• Face detection

• Backside illumination
• iSight camera

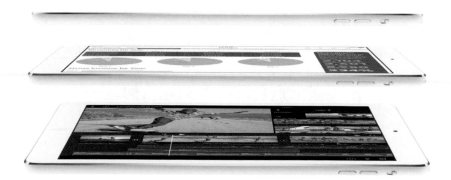

iFACT
The iPad Air is more than a millimetre thinner than the previous iPad which makes a huge difference and that's why it feels so much less bulky.

1080p HD Video Recording

- Tap to focus while recording
- Video stabilization
- Face detection

- Backside illumination
- 3x video zoom

Battery Life

- Up to 10 hours of surfing the web on Wi-Fi, watching video, or listening to music

- Up to 9 hours of surfing the web using cellular data network
- Charging via power adapter or USB to computer system

Siri

- Use your voice to send messages, set reminders, and more.

SIM Card

- Nano-SIM

iPad Air

9

The Anatomy Of An iPad Air

You've no doubt noticed various buttons, sensors, slots and things on your iPad. If you want to know what they're all for and what they all do, we shall reveal all, but not in a naughty way!

1. The Home Button

The Home button is your route back to the home screen at all times. It doesn't matter what you're doing, whether you're shooting a video, playing a game or messing about on Facebook, one press of the Home button returns you to the home screen instantly. Double tapping the Home button brings up the multitasking view where you'll see all your active apps appear as windows at the bottom of the screen. As with everything else, a single tap of the Home button in the multitasking view returns to the home screen. Holding the Home button down for a few moments activates Siri. You can also take a screen capture by holding the Sleep/Wake button and tapping the Home button.

2. The Sleep/Wake Button

This is another control that you'll be using a lot. To turn off your iPad's screen, just press this button, which is tucked away on the edge of your iPad in the top-right hand corner. This is useful if you need to conserve battery power. You can either put your iPad to sleep or, if you won't be using it for a while, you can turn it off by holding down this button for a few seconds until the Slide To Power Off option appears. You can also use the Sleep/Wake button to turn the screen back on when you want to use your iPad again, but if it's only in sleep mode, the Home button will do the same job. If your iPad is powered off, hold the Sleep/Wake button to turn it back on. Holding the Sleep/Wake button and tapping the Home button takes a capture of whatever is on the screen at that moment and saves it to Photos.

3. The +/- Buttons

Pressing the plus and minus buttons while on the home page will increase or decrease the volume respectively. In fact, pressing these buttons will alter the volume of any audio that is currently being played through the speaker or your headphones. The plus button also doubles as a more conveniently placed shutter button to take pictures with your iPad camera.

4. Mute/Lock Orientation

Above the volume buttons on the side of your iPad, you'll find a switch that either mutes the volume or locks the orientation of your iPad. In order to toggle between the two options, you need to visit Settings and look under the General option. Normally, turning your iPad on

"The Retina display on the iPad features a 2048x1536 resolution, rich colour saturation and an astounding 3.1 million pixels"

its side will change the screen orientation from portrait to landscape or vice versa, but you can flick this switch to lock the screen to its current orientation.

5. The Screen

It's a sensitive little screen, so only the lightest touch or the faintest swipe of the finger is needed to achieve the desired effect. The Retina display on the iPad features a 2048x1536 resolution, rich colour saturation and an astounding 3.1 million pixels. That's four times the number of pixels displayed by the iPad 2 and a million more than an HDTV. Those pixels are so close together, your eyes can't discern individual ones at a normal viewing distance. Every iPad also boasts a fingerprint-resistant screen coating to prevent smears, and strengthened glass on both the front and rear panels. It's probably best not to test that strength out by dropping it though, just in case.

6. The Front Camera

With the new FaceTime HD camera, everyone can get an even better view of you and what's around you. You can also use it for taking self-portraits or recording 720p HD video. The front-facing camera is known as the FaceTime camera, because its primary purpose is to enable video calls. The camera is centred above the screen, and can take 1.2-megapixel photographs or 720p HD video.

7. The Rear Camera

The iPad's main camera is called the iSight camera. It can take five-megapixel photos and 1080p HD video. It has a five-element lens and a hybrid IR filter, which might not mean very much if you're not into photography, but suffice it to say that it takes some pretty good quality snaps, whether by sunlight or candlelight. There are a few more handy features built in too, including face detection, to focus on the important part of your photo, and video stabilisation, to smooth out any shakiness in your images.

8. The Microphone

If you're recording video or making a call via FaceTime, it might be useful to know where the microphone is on your iPad, to make sure you get the clearest sound. Well, you'll find it right on the top of your iPad, just above the front-facing camera, so if you are making a FaceTime call, you'll be looking and speaking in the same direction.

9. The Speakers

Unlike the iPhone, which has its speaker at the top so you can hear the person you're talking to when you hold the phone to your ear, the iPad's speakers are at the bottom. This is where you'll hear all the sound from your iPad, whether that's audio during a FaceTime chat, music, sound effects, or dialogue when you're watching a movie.

10. The Lightning Connector Port

When you need to plug your iPad in to charge or to transfer files, you'll need to plug your charger or cable into this tiny port, found at the very bottom of your iPad. The Lightning Connector was introduced with the most recent Apple products; it's smaller and simpler than the previous connector, which used 30 pins. The Lightning Connector has only nine pins and is a completely different shape. If you have an iPad accessory that depends on the 30-pin connector, you can still connect it to your new iPad. Simply use a Lightning to 30-pin Adapter (sold separately).

11. The SIM Port

If your iPad is a Wi-Fi-only model, this won't be there. If you have a 3G/4G + Wi-Fi model, though, turn your iPad over to see the slot where the SIM card is inserted. If you do have this model, you'll find it's a bit fiddly to insert the SIM card in the first place; you'll need to use a pin or the SIM eject tool that came in the box to press the tiny button in the hole on the side, and then the SIM tray will pop out. The SIM enables you to surf the web on the move with a mobile data plan as you would with a mobile phone, while the Wi-Fi only models need to connect to a Wi-Fi service.

Welcome to iOS 7

iOS 7 is the latest version of Apple's mobile operating system. If you're familiar with previous versions of iOS, you'll find it looks rather different and it comes with a whole raft of new features and improvements.

Over the past six years iOS has established itself as one of the world's leading mobile operating systems, but with competition heating up from Google Android, Windows Phone and Blackberry, Apple needed to deliver something special with iOS 7, and they've done so.

The seventh chapter of iOS, the mobile operating system unique to Apple, brings with it a complete overhaul of the user interface. Apple calls the design alterations the "most significant" it has made since iOS debuted in 2007 and it's hard to argue. No feature was exempt, as everything from the Lock Screen to the Safari browser has undergone a facelift, giving the system a fresh and vibrant new look.

Iconography

Apple stood by its word, doing away with 'skeuomorphic' design – which was originally championed by former Apple CEO Steve Jobs – in which icons resemble real-world objects that are instantly recognisable. The newly designed icons are stripped down and lack the detail of their predecessors but they still retain those Apple-like characteristics that users are familiar with. Although the icons have gone flat, they are intelligently enhanced on the homepage by the use of translucency and dynamic wallpapers that move from side-to-side in the background when the device is tilted, giving the screen a sense of depth and an almost three-dimensional feel when tilted.

Apple's goal is for people to know automatically how to navigate and operate an iOS device when they pick it up for the first time and the new design is geared toward that. It also makes accessing your content easier than ever before, enabling you to jump backwards and forwards from page to page with one swipe of a finger. Control Center, which incorporates various shortcuts, the updated Notification Center and the camera are all accessible from the Lock Screen with one simple movement, and these are just a few examples of just how easy it is to move around the iOS environment using these new tools.

The Best Is Now Even Better

While the innovative and unique user interface is the most talked about aspect of iOS 7, there are also plenty of other noteworthy new features. There are updates to security, Siri has become even more intelligent, there are more opportunities to share files swiftly with the implementation of AirDrop and your apps can now automatically update for you, amongst other things.

Your iPad Air, along with the latest iPhones (the 5c and 5s) and the new iPad mini, has been built specifically with iOS 7 in mind and it's fully equipped to take advantage of all the system's awesome features. Now let's take a look at just a few of the things that make iOS 7 unquestionably the best iOS to date.

> "The seventh chapter of iOS, the mobile operating system unique to Apple, brings with it a complete overhaul of the user interface"

iTip – CONTROL CENTER
Don't underestimate the usefulness of Control Center. It's easy to forget it's there but it can be such a time-saver when you start using it.

User Interface Overhaul

Apple says it brought "order to complexity" with the introduction of iOS 7, which brings a long-awaited redesign of the user interface. While the layout of the homepage remains relatively unchanged, the redesigned icons, use of translucency, tweaking of the typography and a new palette of colours give the operating system a clean look, which is easy to navigate.

The Parallax Effect

The new homepage looks almost three-dimensional with the icons, background and application pop ups being built on separate layers giving an illusion of depth to your screen. When you move your device from side-to-side, the dynamic wallpaper brings the screen to life while the icons remain stationary. This parallax effect is also noticeable when you open folders.

Control Center

This feature helps you get where you need to be more quickly. The Control Center is just one swipe away no matter what screen you're on and offers instant access to a hub of controls including Airplane Mode, Wi-Fi, a brightness adjuster and multimedia bar as well as shortcuts to the camera and clock. As of now you're unable to customise what apps appear in the hub.

Notification Center

This feature offers you an at-a-glance view of your day and can now be accessed from any page, including the lock screen, by swiping down. Your notices are conveniently arranged into three tabs – Today, All and Missed – and its more user friendly than before. Notices include birthdays, updates and messages and they can be customised to suit you in Settings.

Welcome to iOS 7 (continued)

Multi-Tasking For All Apps

Battery drainage was often a criticism of multi-tasking, which is accessible by double clicking the home button, but iOS 7 has learnt to track which apps you use the most and when you're likely to use them. So if you usually go on Facebook at lunchtime, your feed will be loaded up at that time. The remainder of the day it will sit in suspended mode to save battery life.

Automatic App Updates

This is one of the new features iOS users will be most pleased with. Gone are those little red warning dots nagging you to update your apps. Now, once switched on in Settings, the App Store will kindly update your apps automatically whenever you're connected to Wi-Fi. When an app has been upgraded it will appear in Notification Center and on App Store updates.

Picture Filters

On the iPhone version of iOS 7 the camera app now has an Instagram-like feel. You can apply various filters to your photos before or after you take a picture and you can also take panoramic shots. Unfortunately these options aren't yet available in the iPad version but we're hopeful they will be added at some point in a future update. Surely!

Photo Organisation

The Photo app now arranges your photos into Years, Collections (albums) and Moments (images) using geotagging, making it easier to scroll through your image bank and find specific snap shots. iCloud Photo Share enables you to share images with friends and family who have iOS devices and they can post videos, pictures and comments on your feed.

iTip – MAPS

After iOS 6's maps debacle, Apple has gone back to the drawing board and the company is now inviting users of iOS 7 to help improve the app.

Safari Updates

A completely redesigned Safari now gives a much more satisfying and complete web browsing experience than ever before. You can now navigate backwards and forwards on any site by simply swiping and a useful new unified search field means URLs and search words can be entered in the same place. Surfing the internet on the move has never been so good.

Shared Links

We live in an age when we no longer need to search for news because the stories find us. With this in mind, Safari has incorporated a very useful Shared Links feature that collates URLs posted on your Twitter feeds and which may have been overlooked. The Shared Links tab in the browser includes the link, who tweeted it and what they said about it. So simple but so cool.

App Store Additions

The App Store boasts more than 800,000 apps and iOS 7 has incorporated new features to make it easier to find what you want. Apps Near Me helps you search for apps that are applicable to the location you're in and parents can now search for age-appropriate apps. Another neat feature enables you to scan gift cards into the App Store with your camera.

AirDrop File Sharing

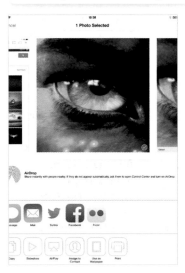

AirDrop is new to iOS 7 and it was featured heavily in Apple's promotional material. It provides an efficient way to share files, including videos, pictures and map links, with people near you whether they're in your contacts book or not and it's "highly secure" says Apple. To use AirDrop you must have an iCloud account and both Wi-Fi and Bluetooth switched on.

iPad Air

Welcome to iOS 7 (continued)

Live Weather Animations

There are a few apps and features of iOS 7 currently missing from the iPad version, and we're sorry to say the weather app is one of them. On the iPhone you get a lovely animated representation of the weather in your current (or selected) location, but inexplicably it's nowhere to be found on the iPad. We can only assume Apple will sort this out at some point.

Siri Updates

The iOS 7 version of Siri continues to add to its unnerving intelligence. There are new commands available, new male and female voices, which will initially be available in English (US), German and French, and you now have the ability to edit your commands with the keyboard. Twitter and Wikipedia have also been added, making Siri a much more powerful option.

Activation Lock

iPads are targets for thieves everywhere and while Find My iPhone (compatible with iPad) went some way to improving security, the Activation Lock should deter pickpockets even further. It requires you to input your Apple ID and password before switching off Find My iPhone and erasing your device and the same details are required to reactivate your device.

iTunes Radio

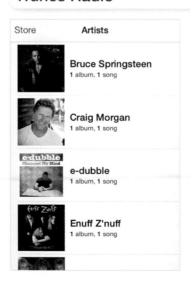

If you live in America then you'll be able to enjoy the benefits of a great new feature in iTunes – iTunes Radio. Unfortunately this feature has yet to be made available to users outside the United States. We understand that Apple is planning to activate iTunes Radio in Europe some time in 2014, so we'll just have to be patient for now. Come on Apple, we're waiting!

iTip – GIFT CARDS
If you receive a gift card, you can now simply import it directly into the App Store by scanning it with the camera on the front of your device.

Contact Blacklist

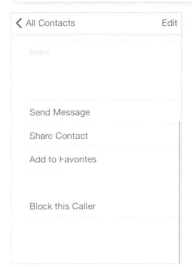

This applies more to iPhone users, but it's relevant to iPad as well. The Contact Blacklist allows you to block someone from contacting you over the phone (on iPhone) or via FaceTime and the various messaging services. You can add people to the list via Settings or within the contact itself, but you can undo your actions at any time if you have a change of heart.

Social Media Sharing

iOS has often come in for criticism for its limited third-party social media integration. Before iOS 7 the only social networks through which you could share photos and images on were Facebook and Twitter but iOS 7 has now incorporated image and video hosting sites Flickr and Vimeo to the sharing options. The limited scope may still disappoint users of other sites but it is an improvement.

iCloud Keychain

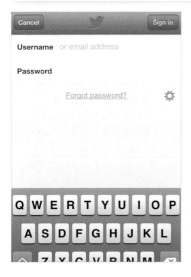

Remembering usernames and passwords is becoming more difficult with the ever-growing list of accounts we subscribe to. Now iCloud Keychain, which has been incorporated into iOS 7, has the ability to remember these things as well as credit card details. If you're out of ideas, Safari can generate unique passwords and store them in the Cloud.

iOS in the Car

This feature (due for release in 2014) will integrate your iOS device with your car, if your vehicle is equipped with iOS. It lets you interact with your iPad via either the controls in your car or Siri, enabling you to play music, dictate messages and make calls. So far 12 car manufacturers are on board including Volvo, Chevrolet and Mercedes.

iPad Air

What Is iCloud?

You may have heard the term 'cloud storage' at some point. If you've no idea what it means, you've come to the right place. Here we clue you in on all you need to know.

iCloud has been around for a couple of years now and it's revolutionised the way we back up our data and store our important information. With around 300 million people using iCloud and the number growing all the time, the service is flying high and it's set to soar even higher in the coming months and years.

Put simply, it's the glue that keeps all your Apple devices stuck together so you can share content between your iPhone, iPad, iPod and Mac. You sign in on any device using your Apple account, and then whatever you've dropped into your iCloud account is available on all the other Apple devices. For example, if a friend has a film stored on their iPhone but you want to watch it on your iPad, log into your iPad with their details and the film's there to watch on the larger screen.

Apple gives each iCloud user 5GB free, not enough to stash your entire film and music library but enough for a few weeks' worth of entertainment. But you can easily upgrade it to 15GB for £14 a year, 25GB for £28 and 55GB for £70.

It's not just about saving media though. It's a brilliant backup system for everything on your iPad including emails, calendar, contacts, applications, photos – pretty much everything on your iPad that you'd want backing up if it were to get lost.

There are now loads of cloud storage providers out there, with Dropbox being the most well known and oldest of the big players. Microsoft's Sky Drive and Google Cloud are two other big players trying to get a bigger slice of this rapidly growing market – but why should you choose iCloud over its rivals? Well, first and foremost it depends on what other devices and software packages you use. If you're a total Applephile (and there are many) that has an iPhone, iPad and a Mac running OS X then for sheer connectivity, iCloud trounces the other cloud services as Apple's various devices are all so well integrated together that they're like one big machine. iCloud isn't so hot if you're a PC user – you can go on www.icloud.com and do things like Find My iPhone, look up contacts and check email, but it doesn't offer PC users anywhere near the same functionality as it does Mac users.

Back Up And More

Even if the only Apple product you own is an iPad, it's worth signing up for as it's free and valuable for backing up your iPad's essential data. If you're a PC user – get Dropbox and while you're at it as there's a brilliant Dropbox app on the App Store. Armed with iCloud and Dropbox you'll be truly connected to the world of cloud storage with the best of all worlds just a tap away.

At its most basic, iCloud is a brilliant data back-up facility, but it can be so much more than that.

How To Use... iCloud

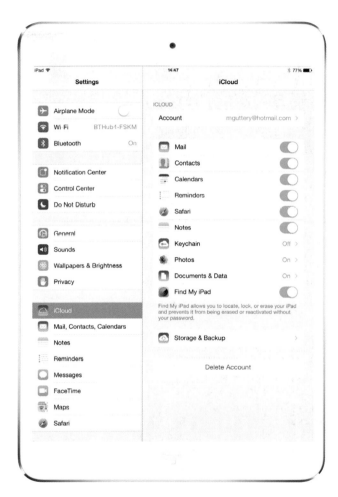

If you're still fuzzy about the concept of cloud storage, don't worry. Follow this tutorial to get it set up and that's that. Once its up and running it takes care of itself all on its own!

Step 1: Getting Started

Yes it's an impressive service, but that doesn't mean it's expensive. Put the wallet away, as a basic iCloud account is actually free. All you need to get started is an Apple ID, but getting one of those is also free. You can sign up for one directly through your iPad, or you can do it through a computer with iTunes installed, preferably the one you'll be linking your iPad to.

Step 2: Creating An iCloud Account

Armed with your trusty Apple ID you can go into the iPad's Settings menu from the home page and scroll down slightly until you find the iCloud section. Touch this and then touch the Apple ID box to bring up the virtual keyboard. Type in the email you used to set up your ID, then enter your password into the box below, tap the large Sign In button and iCloud will then be enabled.

iPad Air

How To Use... iCloud (continued)

Step 3: Merging Your Current Data

After a few seconds while your iPad confirms your login details, you'll get an alert asking to merge your current data. If you haven't used iCloud before, then you won't have anything to merge. However, if you already have iCloud set up on a computer or other iOS device, then agreeing to this will copy across all of your previously saved data over to your iPad.

Step 4: Locating Your Position

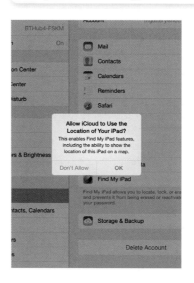

After this, you'll get another alert asking if iCloud can use the location of your iPad. This is important because the Find My iPhone app – which can show your iPad on a map if it gets lost or stolen – won't work unless you accept this. Tap the OK button or you can pick Don't Allow and then just turn the location-based settings on later instead, if you like.

Step 5: Changing Your iCloud Settings

Now you'll see the apps and services that can be linked to your iCloud account. Not surprisingly, you can link or unlink each one simply by flicking the corresponding switch to the on or off position. It's as simple as that. Each one you link will share all data created within it through iCloud to any other linked devices you might own such as an iPhone or iPod.

Step 6: Backing Up Your iPad

At the bottom of the iCloud screen are the Storage & Backup options. Your basic iCloud account can create a backup of your iPad, which can then be used to restore it if something goes wrong. Turn on the iCloud Backup option and it'll do it automatically whenever you plug your iPad into a power source while it's connected up to a wireless network.

iTip – LINKED DOWNLOADS
If you link your app, music and video purchases to iCloud, then anything that you buy from the App or iTunes store automatically downloads to all of your linked devices.

Step 7: Buying More Storage

A free iCloud account comes with 5GB of storage space included. While that doesn't sound like much, it's actually a lot more than you'd think. If it's not quite enough to hold all your documents and data though, you can always add an extra 10, 20 or 50GB for a yearly subscription. Tap Change Storage Plan and then choose from the list that appears if you want to do so.

Step 8: Managing Your iCloud Storage

On the Storage & Backup screen, tapping Manage Storage enables you to see how your iPad's storage is being used. Touching anything on the list reveals more details, along with an Edit button. Use this to delete anything you don't want to keep. You can also edit your backup settings to change what gets backed up and what doesn't. It's entirely up to you.

Step 9: Accessing iCloud On Your iPad

Not surprisingly, accessing any linked content from iCloud is as simple as using the app that it's linked to. Mail accesses emails; Contacts shares your numbers and addresses; Calendar and Reminders transfer appointments, meetings, alarms and alerts; Photos keeps a backup of every picture in your Photo Stream from the last 30 days and so on.

Step 10: Using A Computer With iCloud

Helpfully, you can access certain elements of your iCloud account from any computer, anywhere in the world. Go to **www.icloud.com** and enter your Apple ID email and password, then click one of the five icons - Mail, Contacts, Calendar, Find My iPad or iWork - to access any of the content that you've linked to iCloud.

Your iPad Air And
The Basics

So, you're ready to get started setting up your lovely new iPad Air. There are a few steps that you need to go through before you can start using it properly and we've got a complete step-by-step guide that will get you through the set-up process as painlessly as possible. We also take you through how to set up and use an Apple ID. This is basically the account that identifies you as the owner of your iPad, it enables you to personalise it, purchase apps and more. We also look at how to connect your iPad up to a computer. This is useful for backing up files, apps and settings, and it also enables you to transfer music stored on your computer.

When you've worked through the tutorials in this section, your iPad will be fully up and running and you'll be able to start using it properly, so let's get started and see what it can do!

> "We've got a complete step-by-step guide that will get you through the set-up process as painlessly as possible"

24 How To Set Up Your iPad

- Language And Location
- Setting Up Wi-Fi
- Restoring From A Back-Up
- Signing In With An Apple ID
- Finishing Up
- The Home Page
- Using The Search Page
- Adjusting Settings To Save Battery
- Using Pre-Loaded Apps
- Simple Finger Gestures
- Changing View Orientation
- Setting Up Security
- Restricting iPad Use
- Make It More Accessible

28 How To Use An Apple ID

- Why You Need An Apple ID
- Creating A New Apple ID
- Pick An Email Address
- Getting A Free Email Account
- Finishing Up
- What To Use Your Apple ID For

30 How To Use A Computer With Your iPad

- Downloading iTunes
- Plugging In For The First Time
- General Connection Information
- Choosing Your Media Content
- Syncing Your iPad
- Checking Your iPad Content

How To... Set Up Your iPad

If you're turning on a new iPad for the first time, there is a brief set-up procedure that you'll have to complete in order to get it working. Just follow these steps.

Step 1: Language And Location

Your iPad should come already charged, but it's best to Plug it into the wall using the USB cable and plug adapter provided, then turn it on. Start by choosing your language and location. These may default to specific settings depending on where you bought your iPad. Next, choose Enable Location Services so apps like Maps and Find My iPhone work properly.

Step 2: Setting Up Wi-Fi

Although enabled iPads can use the 3G/4G network to access the Internet, most of us will use Wi-Fi. If you're setting up your iPad in a place with Wi-Fi access, you can detect and configure this on the next screen. Using Wi-Fi is preferable, as it's faster and won't lead to you incurring hefty 3G/4G charges from your service provider if you have a data limit in place.

iTip – AIRPLANE MODE
If you're going on a plane but don't want to turn your iPad off, go into Settings and flick the Airplane Mode switch to On, making your iPad safe for use in flight.

Step 3: Restoring From A Back-Up

After a short activation period you'll get the option to restore from an iCloud or iTunes backup. This is obviously only appropriate if you've previously owned and backed up an iPad – if you haven't, you just need to choose Set Up As A New iPad to continue. Don't worry too much about this and click on through to complete the set up. Obviously, if you have settings backed up, do it.

Step 4: Signing In With An Apple ID

The next screen prompts you to create an Apple ID, which you'll need to use a large number of apps and services on your iPad. If you already have one from using an iPod Touch, iPhone, Mac or previous iPad, you can sign in with it here. If you don't have one though, choose Skip This Step, because we cover how to create an Apple ID for yourself later on in this chapter.

Step 5: Finishing Up

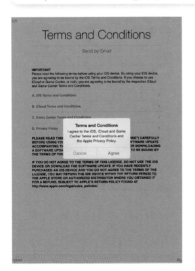

The next few steps are fairly basic, although you still have to do them. There's a terms and conditions page that you can wade though, but it's easier just to press the Agree button (if you press Disagree, you can't use your iPad!). You can also choose to send or not send automatic diagnostic/usage data to Apple. It's entirely up to you and you can come back and change these choices later.

Step 6: The Home Page

After all that you'll eventually arrive at the home screen where all the iPad's apps and services can be found. To return here at any time, press the Home button. You can use your finger to flick left and reveal a second page with more apps. The more apps you add to your iPad, the more screens you'll have to scroll through. Get used to it – you'll be seeing this screen a lot!

How To... Set Up Your iPad (continued)

Step 7: Using The Search Page

Swiping down from the middle of the home page to brings up the search page. You can use this to search your iPad for something specific using keywords, for example an app. Type a word into the search bar using the keyboard and anything that matches (from contacts and emails to music, apps, videos and more) will be shown in a list. Just tap the appropriate result.

Step 8: Adjusting Settings To Save Battery

Since the iPad is demanding in terms of battery usage, it's worth adjusting some of the basic settings to make it last longer. Press the Settings icon, then choose Brightness. You can use the slider to dim the screen and save power, as well as turning on auto-brightness. Go back via the Settings arrow, choose General, then Bluetooth and turn it off.

Step 9: Using Pre-Loaded Apps

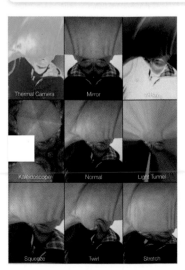

Your iPad already has plenty of apps on it that you can use. To start one, just tap the relevant icon on the home page. Most of these are fully explained in the corresponding tutorials that you'll find later in this guide. Feel free to open the apps up and play around with them. You can't do any harm and this is the best way to get a feel for the iPad if you've never used such a thing before.

Step 10: Simple Finger Gestures

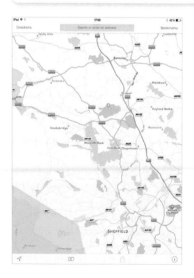

The iPad uses many different finger gestures as control methods. Swiping is easy: touch the screen, then move left, right, up or down to scroll pages, lists and other things that are bigger than the screen. Pinching is used to zoom in and out: using two fingers, touch and then pinch in or stretch out. This is a primary function used by apps like Photos and Maps, amongst others.

iTip – NAME YOUR iPAD
Go to Settings, General, About and touch the Name panel to rename your iPad. This is what will show up when linking to a computer or using personal hotspots.

Step 11: Changing View Orientation

Although the home page of your iPad is locked by default to a portrait (vertical) view, many apps let you turn the iPad on its side and automatically use a landscape (horizontal) view instead. To prevent this perspective switch from happening by accident though, you can lock the portrait view in the Settings menu, under General. Adjust it as circumstances require.

Step 12: Setting Up Security

To set a password to prevent use of your iPad if it's lost or stolen, go to Settings, General, Passcode Lock and tap Turn Passcode On, then select a four-digit passcode. Be sure to remember it! If you turn off Simple Passcode, you can set a more complex password. You can also set your iPad to automatically wipe itself after ten incorrect code entries.

Step 13: Restricting iPad Use

If you allow other people or children to use your iPad, it's wise to set up some restrictions on the use of various apps. Go to Settings, General, Restrictions and tap Enable Restrictions, then flick the switches to either On or Off depending on what you want to lock out. Putting restrictions on adding/deleting apps is a good idea, as is restricting the use of Safari, for added peace of mind.

Step 14: Make It More Accessible

Also in the Settings menu, you'll find some accessibility options. Here, you can set it so that your iPad can read text aloud, or you can make the default text size much bigger. Both of these options might be helpful if your eyesight isn't very good. In the same menu, you'll also find audio and colour settings, so you can make your iPad work in a way that's best for you.

iPad Air

How To Use... An Apple ID

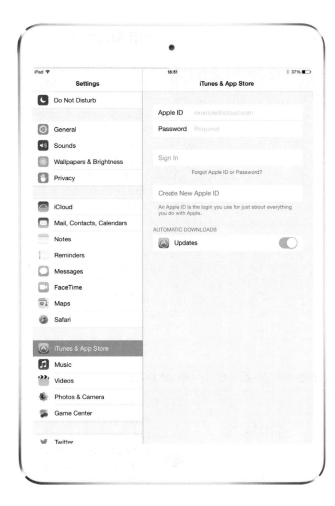

An Apple ID is essential if you want to make the most of your iPad, but thankfully it's very easy to set one up. Here's how to create one for yourself.

Step 1: Why You Need An Apple ID

It's perfectly possible to get by without having an Apple ID, but you'll be missing out on a lot of content (and some apps won't even work properly!). Without one, you can't use the App Store, iTunes, iCloud and a lot of other apps, so it's worth setting one up immediately. It's totally free and it only takes a couple of minutes, and you can even do it directly through your iPad.

Step 2: Creating A New Apple ID

There are several apps that prompt you to create a new Apple ID (such as the App Store, for instance), but it's easiest to do it through iCloud. Go to Settings, iCloud and tap Get A Free Apple ID at the bottom. This brings up a screen asking for your date of birth. Enter it and then press Next to move to the next screen where you'll be prompted to enter your full name.

iTip – DELETE ACCOUNT
Don't worry about pressing the red Delete Account button at the bottom of the iCloud settings. It will delete it from your iPad, it won't delete the account from existence!

Step 3: Pick An Email Address

Next, you'll be asked to choose whether to use your current email address to sign up or create a new iCloud email address. If you want to use your existing email address, choose that option and press Next. The next screen will prompt you to enter your email address, and then you can press Next and carry on filling in the rest of your details (including setting a password).

Step 4: Getting A Free Email Account

If you don't have an email account already or you want to set up a fresh one specifically for your iPad, you can get a free @icloud.com account directly from Apple. Select the Get A Free @icloud.com Email Address option and type what you'd like it to be into the box below. Try to make it unique, because if that address is already in use, you'll have to start the process all over again.

Step 5: Finishing Up

You'll be asked for a few more details, and then the terms and conditions will appear. Agree to these and you're done! If you chose to create an @icloud.com email address, that account is now added to your iPad's Email app; if you used an existing one, you'll need to check the inbox for that address for a confirmation email and click the link to verify it as yours before iCloud will be activated.

Step 6: What To Use Your Apple ID For

With your Apple ID set up, you can use your iPad to do plenty of things. For instance, if you're going to use it to play games, it's well worth going into the Game Center app and entering your Apple ID details to create a profile that'll store your gaming progress. Most importantly, don't forget that you'll need an activated Apple ID to buy apps from the App Store.

iPad Air

How To Use... A Computer With Your iPad

Your iPad can be used completely independently of a computer but connecting it up enables you to back up content, restore settings and add music ripped from CDs. Here's how to connect your iPad to a PC or Mac.

Step 1: Downloading iTunes

In order to have your computer recognise your iPad and be able transfer files between the two, you'll have to install iTunes first. It's a free download and acts as the management software between your media and your iPad. Go to www.apple.com/itunes and click Free Download, then follow the instructions to get the right version.

Step 2: Plugging In For The First Time

Once you've installed iTunes, use the USB charging cable to connect your iPad to your computer and it should open automatically. You'll now get to rename your iPad and have the option to switch auto-syncing on or off. If you download apps through iTunes on your computer, this will automatically add them to your iPad too.

iTip – EJECTING YOUR iPAD
When you're ready to disconnect your iPad from your computer, always be sure to press the eject button shown under the Devices heading before unplugging it!

Step 3: General Connection Information

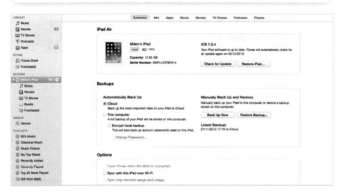

The summary screen shows all the basic information about your iPad, including a breakdown of what's on it and how much space it's taking up. From here, you can change the backup settings between iCloud and your computer, activate backup over Wi-Fi and also say whether iTunes opens automatically when you plug it in.

Step 4: Choosing Your Media Content

Each tab across the top represents things you can add to your iPad. Info relates to things like your calendar, reminders and contacts, Photos obviously mean your photos and the rest are things that can be purchased from the Apple App Store. Music and video can also be added from your own private collection if you so wish.

Step 5: Syncing Your iPad

Whenever you plug your iPad in and start iTunes, it'll sync, so any content on your iPad that isn't on your computer will automatically copy itself over for safe keeping. To send content to your iPad instead, choose what to send in the various tabs and then click Apply button in the bottom-right corner to get the transfer going.

Step 6: Checking Your iPad Content

For more information about what's on your iPad, click on the media categories in the left column. Links to Music, Films, TV Programmes and so on appear here, and by clicking on each of these you can see exactly what's on your iPad. To see which apps are on your iPad, you'll need to click the Apps tab at the top.

Your iPad Air And
Customisation

Customisation is an integral part of the iPad experience. You can customise pretty much everything about your device from the way it looks to the way you interact with it, not to mention the way it interacts with you. You can set up alerts and notifications for the apps and services you're interested in. We also guide you through using folders to organise your apps. We explain how to use the App Store to purchase and download apps and also how to remove apps that you don't want. Of course, the more apps you download, the more cluttered your home screens will become and before you know it you won't be able to find anything. That's where folders come in. They enable you to group similar apps together and our tutorial explains how to create and use them to organise your apps effectively.

To help you get the look and feel you want, we've gathered together some of our favourite customisation apps from the App Store. Customisation isn't just about changing the background wallpaper, it's about making your iPad work for you in the most efficient way.

"You can customise pretty much everything about your device from the way it looks to the way you interact with it"

How To... Change The Wallpaper

The most obvious way to personalise your iPad environment is by changing the lock and home screen wallpapers. Here's how to do it.

Step 1: Wallpaper Positions

For anyone unfamiliar with the term, 'wallpaper' refers to the background picture on an electronic device display - the decoration, if you like. There are two wallpaper slots on the iPad that you can change to give your tablet a bit more character – the home screen and the lock screen. Unlike previous versions of iOS, iOS 7 even enables you to have animated wallpapers as well.

Step 2: Stock Wallpapers

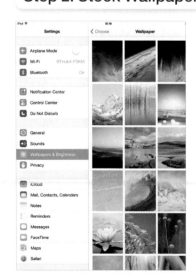

The iPad actually comes pre-loaded with a fairly large (if rather boring) selection of stock wallpapers that you can apply to either the home or lock screen (or both), which you can find by going to the Settings menu, tapping the Wallpapers & Brightness option and then Choose Wallpaper. They're all the right size for the iPad display, so they can't be resized when you apply them.

iTip – SCREEN CAPTURING
You can save an image of the iPad screen to Photos at any time by pressing the sleep/wake button and the home button simultaneously.

Step 3: Custom Wallpapers

It's also possible to apply any image you choose as wallpaper, provided that it's already been saved in your Camera Roll folder. This obviously applies to photographs that you take yourself, but also to images that you have saved from the Internet. This custom option also lets you resize your images by zooming in or out, as well as moving it around to focus on a specific chosen part of the image.

Step 4: Download Your Own Images

To get images from the Internet, load up Safari and use the Google Search box in the top-right corner to search for anything you like, for example 'ipad wallpapers', by typing it in. There are plenty of perfectly sized options that look great for you to choose from. When you find one you want, open it in the browser window and hold your finger down, choose Save Image when the option appears.

Step 5: Applying Images As Wallpaper

To apply an image, all you need to do is go to the Wallpaper option in the Settings menu and tap Choose to select where the image is coming from. When applying custom images, you can move and scale the image first. Drag it around with your finger, and pinch to zoom in or out. When you're happy, select one of the options from Set Lock Screen, Set Home Screen or Set Both, which are all self-explanatory.

Step 6: More Wallpapers

When you've made your selection, your new home page and/or lock screen image will be set. You can change them at any time by following the same steps. Another good source of high quality wallpapers is the App Store. Search for wallpaper apps on there and you'll find a whole load of apps to choose from in a wide range of styles and genres. You could have a new wallpaper every day!

How To... Add And Delete Apps

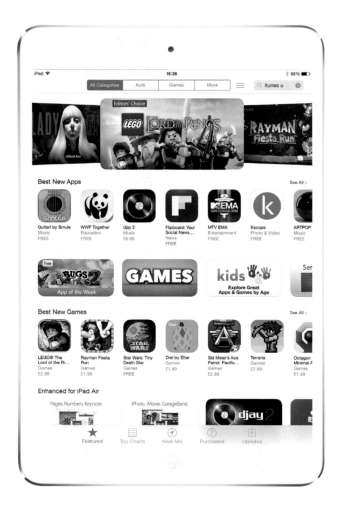

The iPad Air is a beautiful thing, but it's nothing without apps. The App Store is home to hundreds of thousands of apps for almost anything you can imagine.

Step 1: Welcome To The App Store

The place to get your apps is the App Store. You can think of it as a real department store, with products in every category you can think of. You can browse the App Store on a computer through iTunes or on any other iOS device. If you're looking on your iPad, it will filter only apps optimised for the format. So, without further ado lets get you started downloading apps for yourself.

Step 2: Your Account

If you've already created an Apple ID, you'll have instant access to the App Store. However, you have to provide payment details in order to buy apps. Go to Settings then choose iTunes & App Store, touch your Apple ID at the top, select View Apple ID, then tap Payment Information. Enter your card details and address exactly as they're shown on your card statements, then press Done.

iTip – GONE BUT NOT FORGOTTEN
Any app you delete can be re-downloaded from the App Store. Just tap Updates, then the Purchased tab and the Not On This iPad tab to see a full list.

Step 3: Browse The App Store

If we're brutally honest, the App Store is a bit of a nightmare to navigate. Yes, it's split into various genre categories (and further subcategories in some cases) and yes, you can browse via paid apps, free apps and release date headings, but that doesn't mean the best apps are going to be immediately obvious. That doesn't mean you shouldn't have a look though.

Step 4: Search The App Store

If you know the name of an app that you want, you can tap the search icon at the bottom and type it into the field provided. Tap Search and when the list appears, touch an app to read more. As there are many similarly named apps, double-check you've found the one you actually want before you download it. You can also search by keyword if you want to.

Step 5: Downloading Apps

Once you're absolutely sure you've found an app you want, scroll to the top of the information screen and press the button indicating the price (either free or a value). Press it again when it switches to either Install or Buy, then enter your Apple ID password as directed by the pop-up box. The app will then automatically be downloaded to your home page.

Step 6: Deleting Apps

To remove apps you no longer want, go to the home page and hold your finger down on any app icon until they all start jiggling. Now you can browse your home pages and touch the X on any icon to delete that app, confirming your choice before it deletes. Note you can't delete apps that came pre-loaded on the iPad. Only those downloaded from the App Store can be removed.

How To... Create And Use Folders

Folders enable you to keep your ever-expanding app collection organised and neat. After all, the more apps you download, the harder it gets to keep track of them all. Putting them into folders keeps things much more manageable.

Step 1: Why Use Folders?

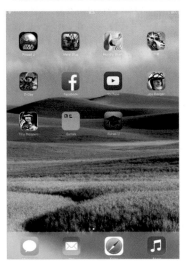

Each time you download a new app, it appears on your home screen. This isn't a problem at first, but the more you download, the more home screens become filled up until you don't know where you are. That's why it's better to put apps into folders. That way you can group similar apps together, which makes it much easier to find them quickly and they take up less space.

Step 2: Making Folders

You can make a folder from the home page. Hold your finger down on any app icon until they all jiggle, then drag any app on top of another. Let go and it'll create a folder with both apps inside. You can then drag another app onto the same folder to place it inside. A single folder can hold as many apps as you like, unlike iOS 6, where the number was limited to 12.

Step 3: Naming Folders

A newly created folder will name itself by default according to the category of the first app it contains. However, you can rename a folder as anything you want simply by opening it, then tapping the text field above it while in edit mode. Type your new name for the folder, then tap Done to confirm. To exit the edit mode, all you have to do is press the home button once.

Step 4: Removing Folders

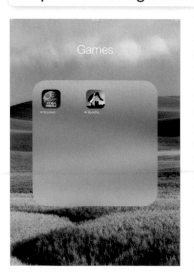

To view the contents of a folder on the home page, just tap it once and it'll open. If you want to remove apps from a folder, touch/hold on any of the app icons until they jiggle to enter edit mode, then drag the app out of the folder. If you move all but one of the apps out of a folder, the folder will be deleted and the space will instead be taken up by the last remaining app in the folder.

How To Use... Multitasking

You may find that you want to switch quickly between different apps. iOS 7 enables you to do this thanks to its handy multitasking feature. While in any given app, all your other apps will be working away in the background.

Step 1: What Is Multitasking?

Multitasking on the iPad seems obvious, but it hasn't been around as long as you'd think. It was only introduced in iOS 4 and before that only certain apps could be run simultaneously. Now though, the iPad can run multiple apps at the same time. You can leave apps running in the background, and even have apps you're not using send you notifications to show things like new emails or Facebook replies.

Step 2: Using Multiple Apps At Once

Using multiple apps is a no-brainer. If you're using an app and want to use another, simply tap the home button and select the new app from the home page instead. The other app will still be running in the background. While you can theoretically have an infinite number of apps open at once, too many can cause your iPad to slow down, so it's not a good idea to leave everything running all the time.

Step 3: Switching Between Apps

When multiple apps are running, there are two different ways of switching between them. One is simply choosing the app that you want from the home page; if it's already running, it'll open up exactly where you left it. Alternatively, double tap the home button to bring up the multitasking bar, and flick left or right to scan through the apps that are currently running, then touch the one you want to open it.

Step 4: Closing Apps

An important thing that many people forget is how to close down apps when you're done using them. Just hitting home may make you think they're shut, but they're still there in the background. To close an app properly, double tap the home button to bring up the multitasking view, then scroll across to find the app you want to close. You can then close it down by swiping it away upwards on the screen.

iPad Air

Your iPad Air And
The Internet

The iPad Air's gorgeous retina display and touch screen combined with iOS 7's much improved Safari web browser make it an absolute pleasure to surf the internet. Whether you're watching videos, posting on forums and message boards or just catching up on the latest news, there's no better way to do it. We've got a tutorial that takes you through a few of Safari's cool features which are sure to improve your browsing experience. We've also got a selection of top internet-related apps for you to have a look at, including a few alternative browsers if you find Safari doesn't meet your needs.

"Whether you're watching videos, posting on forums and message boards or just catching up on the latest news, there's no better way to do it"

42 How To Use Safari

- Opening A Web Page
- Opening Multiple Pages At Once
- Opening Web Links
- Using The Reading List
- Adding Bookmarks
- Important Safari Settings

44 Internet Apps

- Atomic Web Browser
- Free Wi-Fi Finder
- Dolphin Browser
- SpeedTest.net Mobile
- Opera Mini Browser
- Google Drive
- QR Reader For iPad
- PERFECT Web Browser
- Chrome Browser
- Pocket

How To Use... Safari

Safari is Apple's own web browser and versions of it appear on all internet-enabled Apple devices. The iOS 7 version features many enhancements, making it the most powerful mobile Safari yet.

Step 1: Opening A Web Page

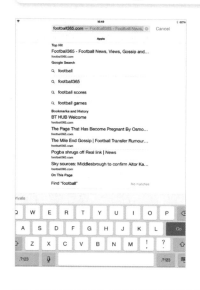

After opening Safari, tap on the text field at the top of the screen. You can type anything in here from keywords to web addresses. iOS 7 is clever enough to distinguish between the two, that's why you don't need separate fields for searches and URLs. Type in the address or whatever else you want to search for and hit the Go key and your page or results will then be displayed.

Step 2: Opening Multiple Pages At Once

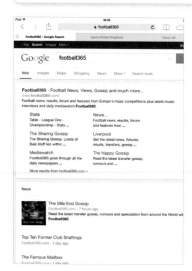

To open a new web page without closing the one you're looking at, tap the plus symbol at the top right of the screen. Your new page will then appear in a new tab. When you have multiple pages open, tap the tabs to switch quickly between them. You can also drag them to change their positions in the tab bar and close tabs quickly by tapping the cross button in the appropriate tab.

iTip – PRIVATE BROWSING
Tap the search bar to bring up the keyboard and you'll see a button that says Private just above it. Tap this to toggle private browsing on and off.

Step 3: Opening Web Links

If you want to open a link from any website that leads to another page within it or even another site entirely, just touch it and it'll load up straight away. However, if you want to open it in a new window, touch and hold your finger on the link. You'll get options including Open in New Tab, Copy (which will copy the link to the pasteboard) and you can also add the page to your reading list.

Step 4: Using The Reading List

You can also add pages to your Reading List by touching the arrow icon and choosing Add to Reading List. To see the Reading List, press the book button and then choose Reading List by touching the glasses icon. You'll see all your saved pages, which are deleted as you read them. These pages will be saved so that you can read them later even without an Internet connection.

Step 5: Adding Bookmarks

Unlike Reading List additions, bookmarks are permanent markers that can be placed on favourite pages making them quick and easy to access. Open a page you want to bookmark, press the arrow button and choose Bookmark. Tapping the book button at the top of the screen then opens a list of all your existing Bookmarks. To open a bookmarked page, just touch it.

Step 6: Important Safari Settings

Go into the Settings menu and scroll down to find Safari. Touch it to access Safari's options. You can change the default search engine, clear your browsing history and clear any saved data such as cookies or passwords. It's best, though, to leave all options under Security (near the bottom) set to on. When you're happy with your settings, hit the home button to back out.

iPad Air

Internet Apps

Browsing the internet on the iPad is a joy, and here are a few apps that can help to make the experience even more joyous still. Check out the App Store for lots more like these.

Atomic Web Browser

Price: £1.49
Developed By: RichTech
In-app Purchases: No

If you're considering an alternative to Safari, Atomic is one of the best non-Apple browsers around. It's designed for touch-screen devices, making use of a series of gestures for control - though it also lets you choose which of 30 available buttons you want to add to it. If you want to try it without handing over your money, there's a free Lite version available too.

Free Wi-Fi Finder

Price: Free
Developed By: JiWire Inc
In-App Purchases: No

Using a 3G network is fine most of the time, but if you need to use larger amounts of data (or you have a tight limit on your mobile contract), then Wi-Fi's the way to go. By using this app, you can discover the location of free Wi-Fi spots almost anywhere in the world. Just follow the map, connect and then get downloading fast.

Dolphin Browser

Price: Free
Developed By: Dolphin Browser
In-App Purchases: No

It's not all about Safari – you can download other web browsers for the iPad too. This one does exactly what it says on the tin, well, apart from the dolphin bit, because that's probably illegal. Browse the web, simplify pages into text form, use gesture control, open pages using easy-to-navigate tabs and more – it's simple, but it does the job.

SpeedTest.net Mobile

Price: Free
Developed By: Ookla
In-App Purchases: No

Reckon your iPad's Internet connection is running a little slow? Find out exactly how fast it's going with this free app. It's quick and easy to use. You just press a button and it tests your download, upload, and ping speeds in less than a minute. It can also let you know if your speeds are inconsistent, and it keeps track of your previous connection speeds so you can see if things are getting better (or worse!) over time.

Opera Mini Browser

Price: Free
Developed By: Opera Software
In-App Purchases: No

Yet another web browser for the iPad, this one's based on the fairly popular Opera browser for home computers and is designed for both high-speed surfing and data saving. There's even a built-in data usage meter designed specifically for people surfing the Internet, since you can use it to see how much of your precious data limit you're using up while browsing out and about.

Google Drive

Price: Free
Developed By: Google Inc.
In-App Purchases: No

Google Drive is a cloud storage service with a difference. With Google Drive you can store all your files in one place, so you can access them from anywhere and share them with any of your contacts. Use the Google Drive app to create, edit, access and share your photos, documents, videos and other files. It's similar to Dropbox and a great alternative storage solution.

QR Reader For iPad

Price: Free
Developed By: TapMedia Ltd
In-app Purchases: No

Even if you don't know what a QR code is, the chances are you'll have seen lots of them, maybe without realising it. A QR code looks like a white square filled with pixelly dots. It's similar in essence to a barcode in that it stores information that can be scanned and decoded electronically. The advantage of QR codes over barcodes is that they're able to store significantly more information. They're becoming increasingly common now and the ability to scan them yourself can be a great time-saver, enabling you to record information in moments. To do so you'll need a QR scanner app and QR Reader for iPad is one of the best around. It's incredibly simple to use. The first time you open up the app, you'll be taken through a step-by-step guide to how it works, which you can read through or skip. If there's anything you don't understand, you can refer back to this at any time. Then it's basically a case of pointing the viewfinder and letting QR Reader do its thing.

If you're looking for a QR scanner then look no further. If this is the first time you've heard of QR codes then now's your chance to get with it.

PERFECT Web Browser

Price: £0.69
Developed By: Vivek Javvaji
In-app Purchases: No

There are many different web browsers available for the iPad, but PERFECT Web Browser is one of the best. It rolls all the things you'd want from a web browser into one package – bookmarks, the ability to view multiple pages, fast loading – and does it in an easy-to-use and flexible fashion. Want to open hundreds of web pages at once without affecting internet speed, or sync your bookmarks? No problem. From optimal memory management to multi-touch commands, it's got a huge amount of power behind it. Well worth a download.

Chrome Browser

Price: Free
Developed By: Google Inc.
In-app Purchases: No

As you might expect from a browser designed by Google, Chrome really is excellent at what it does. Sign in to your Google account to sync Chrome with the desktop version and get all your bookmarks and settings across all your devices. Send pages from your computer to your iPad with one click and read them on the go, even when you're offline. Open and quickly switch between an unlimited number of browser tabs and flip through them with a swipe. Chrome is fast, stable and versatile, an ideal mobile browser by the biggest name in browsing.

Pocket

Price: Free
Developed By: Idea Shower
In-app Purchases: No

Pocket can save your chosen web pages and then let you view them whenever you like, even if you don't have an internet connection on your iPad – handy when you're going on journeys or leaving the grid. Just bring up the page you want to read later in a web browser, then save it to Pocket – the clue's in the title. There's also a Pro version available for £1.99 that lets you view images and web videos at a later date as well. It's a great way to store reading material and and interesting articles that you don't neccessarily have time to read at the time.

Your iPad Air And
Entertainment

The iPad is a wonderful thing, capable of performing many serious and practical functions. For many users though, first and foremost it's an entertainment centre. You can play games on it, listen to music with it, read books and magazines on it and watch TV and movies as well. This section will get you started and it won't be long before you can fully realise the iPad's enormous potential as source of entertainment. We have tutorials on how to add videos to your iPad, how to stream live TV and how to use two of the most popular entertainment apps available – BBC iPlayer and YouTube.

Of course, if it's entertainment you want then you really don't need to look any further than the App Store. It's packed with apps that are guaranteed to provide hours of amusement. We've selected just a few of our favourites to give you a flavour of what's available.

> "If it's entertainment you want then you really don't need to look any further than the App Store. It's packed with apps that are guaranteed to provide hours of amusement"

iPad Air

How To... Buy And Rent Videos On iTunes

You can buy music on iTunes, everyone knows that, but did you know you can also rent and buy movies and TV shows as well? You didn't? Well you do now, and here's how.

Step 1: Browsing The iTunes Video Store

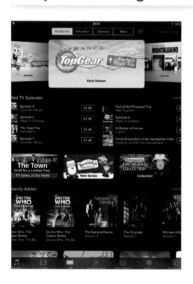

Open iTunes and look at the row of icons along the bottom of the screen. You'll see a Films icon and one for TV programmes. Tap either of them to open the catalogue. You can browse films or TV by category, or search by title, actor or director via the search field at the top right of the screen. When you find a film or TV show you're interested in, simply touch its name.

Step 2: Previewing Videos

Previews are available for more TV shows, while most films have trailers available that you can watch before paying money to rent or buy them. It's a good way to find out whether you'll like something, but be aware that the clip might take a while to load, depending on your Internet connection. It's worth noting, too, that prices vary between high-definition (HD) and standard-definition video.

iTip – STORAGE SPACE
A 45-minute TV episode in HD takes up about 1.4GB of space and a 90-minute film uses about 3GB. Make sure there's space on your iPad before downloading.

Step 3: Buying TV Shows

When buying TV shows, note that they're often cheaper to buy as a series, rather than individual episodes. You can buy most episodes either in high or standard definition, but be careful – HD content will gobble up a lot of your precious storage space, so you might not be able to fit a whole series on your iPad in one go. Keep this in mind.

Step 4: To Buy Or To Rent?

Unlike TV shows, movies can be either rented or purchased, usually in both standard or high definition (which is better but bigger). You can also see a list of other films that viewers also bought in a similar style or genre by opening the 'Related' tab. If you're looking for something new to download or just want inspiration, these lists are well worth a browse.

Step 5: Get Ratings and Reviews

If you're still not sure about whether you want to buy something, you can find out what other people thought of it by opening the Reviews tab. You'll see an overall rating based on all the ratings that have been submitted, and if you scroll down you can see more detailed reviews. Once you've watched something, you might like to leave your own rating and review too. Just a thought.

Step 6: Monitoring Your Downloads

HD content can take time to download and is best done over Wi-Fi. If you're moving out of Wi-Fi range, press the pause button to suspend the download until you get back. Once the download is complete you can go to the Video app to watch it. Then when you sync your device, a standard-definition copy will often be downloaded to your PC or Mac for backup purposes.

How To Use... TV-On-The-Go Apps

It's not just music and gaming that have gone portable thanks to Apple. The rise in on-the-go TV apps for the iPad means it's possible to catch your favourite shows in any place, at any time.

BBC iPlayer spawned an entire generation of 'TV on demand' services. iPlayer paved the way and now most major broadcasters provide TV on the move through dedicated apps. TV on demand was once the exclusive domain of computers, but now you can watch TV anywhere using your iPad.

While it's easy enough to catch the latest soaps and dramas, sports and some other live events tend to get left out of catch-up TV scheduling due to licensing issues (although there are ways around that if you find the right app). Mostly, though, you can find an almost full viewing schedule of either catch-up or live TV to enjoy and, even better, most of these apps are free to use. Indeed, only services like Netflix and LoveFilm require a monthly subscription to use.

Although some services allow you to watch content over a 3G connection – such as iPlayer – most restrict you to a Wi-Fi connection to avoid excessive data charges from mobile providers. Apps from commercial broadcasters tend to come with advertisements, but that really is a small price to pay for the service you receive and you can't expect to get something for nothing.

More For Less

The likes of Netflix and LoveFilm are challenging traditional TV services by offering a wide selection of movies and older TV shows that you can watch whenever you want for a small monthly fee (currently around £5.99, with a one month free trial period). These services work across all your devices including computers, games consoles and Internet-ready TVs, so you can watch a movie on one device and pick it up on the iPad app later on.

Streaming services often have special offers or voucher codes that you can enter on their websites or through the official apps to get additional free content. For instance, LoveFilm is owned by Amazon and if you join via the Amazon site, it is (at the time of writing) offering a free Amazon gift certificate just for trying out the service, which you can use to buy an iTunes voucher for even more content, which is pretty good.

Since these apps all work on iPad, iPod Touch and iPhone, you can also share films and TV content with the family; if one person is hogging the big screen, there's something to keep

Above: BBC iPlayer pioneered on-demand catch up TV and makes a wealth of BBC programming available.

"The likes of Netflix and LoveFilm are challenging traditional TV services by offerings a wide selection of movies and older TV shows for a small monthly fee"

Above: Subscription-based on-demand service Netflix is a great source for films and TV shows.

"With so much content available from so many different apps, the iPad is rapidly becoming a pivotal part of how we watch television these days"

today. More HD content is already being added to these apps and with an iPad HDMI connector (or via AirPlay and an Apple TV box), you can stream 720p HD content to your television, turning your iPad into an HD video player.

The Sky's The Limit

Another app that shows a service provider breaking away from its traditions is Sky Go. Originally available to existing Sky subscribers only, it can now be accessed by anyone; all you need is a Sky Go Monthly Ticket, which is available at various price levels depending on how much you want to watch. Just the basic Sky channels cost around £15 a month, while you can add sports and movies for around £40 (not much less than the proper Sky package).

The latest version of the app adds Sky Atlantic to the list of channels and it offers the ability to watch over a 3G network as well as Wi-Fi. What's more, users can have up to two different devices per account, so you can run the app on your iPad, or use the desktop version to watch your Sky shows on as well as an on an iPhone. And, of course, Sky subscribers get all this included with their existing package; they just have to log into the app with their Sky ID.

With so much content available from so many different apps, the iPad is rapidly becoming a pivotal part of how we watch television these days. As content providers realise the potential of the iPad, you can expect even more apps and shows to be made available in the future. You'll literally be able to watch what you want, when you want, where you want. The future of TV-on-the-go is bright!

everyone else happy too. Even better, if you have an Apple TV unit, then you can play content from the iPad with Netflix in HD and with 5.1 digital surround sound (when available) for that big-screen experience.

Of course, as these services become more established, even more recent and relevant content will be added to make them indispensable. With a huge number of categories and cult films, they form one of the fastest growing media industries

iPad Air

51

How To Use... BBC iPlayer

With BBC iPlayer you can watch any of the existing BBC channels via a live stream, or if there's a programme you missed, almost all the previous week's programming is available to download and view on demand.

Step 1: Using iPlayer

The iPlayer is divided into three main tabs. The Featured tab shows off the BBC's top content of the moment with a list of the latest episodes; Most Popular shows many of the same programmes but in order of viewer popularity; while On Now enables you to see immediately what's on all BBC channels and to start watching live TV right away. It's just like turning on your TV, but even easier.

Step 2: Finding Live TV On iPlayer

You can also use the TV Guide tab to watch live streaming television. The current programme being broadcast will appear first and (if it's being streamed on iPlayer) will have a 'Live' tag. Tap that and you can watch what everyone else is watching on their big screens right on your iPad. Alternatively, drag the date bar to look at older content you might want to watch.

Step 3: Watching Live Television

When you're watching a live broadcast, the 'Live' tag will appear at the bottom. Unlike TiVo or Sky+, you can't pause live shows on your iPad. Hitting pause means you'll rejoin at the current live point. You can find other shows currently airing live by tapping Live Channels in the lower-right corner. Use the arrow in the upper right to maximise the video and tap 'Done' to finish watching.

Step 4: Information On Catch-Up TV

When you choose a show that's already been broadcast from the Channels list, you'll see some detailed information about the programme, including how many days are remaining before it's removed from the iPlayer schedules and a list of similar shows that you might like to view listed below. Tap play to start watching the show you've chosen.

iTip – DON'T LEAVE IT TOO LONG
Don't forget that shows have a limited life on the iPlayer, so you might not be able to watch something really old unless it's been repeated on the BBC recently.

Step 5: Catch-Up TV

Unlike shows broadcast live on iPlayer, you can stop catch-up content at any point and then come back to it later by tapping the pause button on the lower bar. If you have a hearing impairment or just need some help catching some of the noisier segments of a show, many shows have closed subtitles. You can toggle them on and off by tapping the 'S' button at the top of the screen.

Step 6: Radio On iPlayer

You can also listen to BBC radio on the iPlayer and this works in a very similar way to TV, only with stations instead of channels. Navigate to any BBC national station – or a date/show in the catch-up period – that you want to view and you can listen to a recorded programme. And naturally, the iPlayer also lets you tune into radio shows that are currently being broadcast live on air.

Step 7: Adding Shows To Favourites

If you don't want to miss a future episode of a show, you can add it to your favourites by tapping the star in the programme window or by swiping a programme in TV Guide view and tapping the star that appears. All further episodes will then appear on the Favourites page, making it easier for you to manage the programmes you want to watch in future.

Step 8: Parental Control

If you have kids and you're concerned about them stumbling upon inappropriate content, you can set Parental Guidance Lock. Tap the More button at the bottom of the screen and then tap Parental Guidance. You'll be asked to set up a PIN and enter a secret question and answer. After you've done so, content unsuitable for under-16s will be locked safely away.

How To Use... YouTube

The YouTube app does exactly what you'd expect of it. It makes searching for and watching videos as simple as it could possibly be.

Step 1: Watching Videos

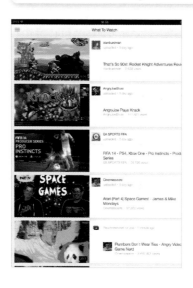

The YouTube app is available from the App Store and is really very simple to use. When you load it up, YouTube will suggest videos you might like to watch. If there are none you're interested in, just keep scrolling down to load more and when you do see one that takes your fancy, touch the preview image to play it. When you've seen enough, just swipe the video screen down and away.

Step 2: Information And Subscribing

When you watch any video on YouTube you will be able to see further details underneath. These include a description of the video, how many times it's been viewed, how many likes it's had and the username of the uploader. You can subscribe to the uploader's channel to receive updates whenever they add new videos, but you'll need to be signed in.

iTip – FOR BEST RESULTS, SIGN IN

You don't need a YouTube account to use the app, but you won't be able to interact or access any of the cooler features unless you sign in.

Step 3: Rate And Comment On Videos

YouTube comments are an important part of the YouTube experience and are famed for the heated exchanges that develop. If you want to join in the fun, tap on the Comments tab and give them a piece of your mind. For a more laconic way of showing your appreciation or otherwise, you can tap the video pane to give it a simple thumbs up or thumbs down. The choice is yours.

Step 4: Bookmarking Videos

Any good videos you find can be saved or shared with your friends by tapping the video and then the plus icon that appears below it. Choose Add to Favourites or Add to Playlist to save it for viewing at a later date. Tapping Share allows you to make it known to your friends either through an email, on Twitter or via any of the other sharing options that are available.

Step 5: Searching For Videos

Searching for videos in the YouTube app is very simple. Just type the name of the video you're looking for or any relevant key words in the search box at the top and you'll be given a list of results matching your search, then tap one of the videos to watch it. To go back to the list of search results, tap the arrow button or swipe down to minimise the video window. Swipe it off the screen to close it.

Step 6: Finding The Best Videos

More browsing options are to be found on the front screen by tapping the menu icon (the one with three horizontal lines) at the top. You can search in different categories, like music or sport, or you can browse the most popular videos on YouTube. To use the sharing options and to comment you'll have to create a YouTube account, in which case your subscribed accounts appear here.

iPad Air

Entertainment Apps

Your iPad is a complete portable entertainment system with loads of apps that are guaranteed to keep you amused where ever you may roam. Here are a few to give you a taste of what's available.

Radio Alan

Price: £0.99
Developed By: BBC Worldwide
In-app Purchases: No

Steve Coogan's Alan Partridge is back, bigger than ever, and you can enjoy some classic Partridge with this app, which mixes your music playlist into Alan's show from Radio Norfolk. If the app recognises tunes in your playlist, Alan will even introduce them on air. If you love Partridge, you're going to love this. Coogan is right on form and at his best.

Fonejacker

Price: £0.69
Developed By: Widebeam Digital
In-app Purchases: No

Prank your friends with the official Fonejacker app, featuring soundboards of your favourite characters voiced by 'Fonejacker' Kayvan Novak, combining classic catchphrases with new quotes exclusive to the app. Characters like art critic Brian Badonde, wheeler dealer Terry Tibbs and Mr Internet Service Providings appear for your amusement.

IMDb Movies & TV

Price: Free
Developed By: IMDb
In-app Purchases: No

IMDb (Internet Movie Database) is often described as the film lovers' bible. What started in 1990 as one film fan's list of favourite movies has grown into one of the most respected websites on the Internet. It's an invaluable resource and a treasure trove for anyone seeking information about anyone at all in the entertainment industry.

StumbleUpon!

Price: Free
Developed By: StumbleUpon
In-app Purchases: No

StumbleUpon! is all about stuff. Cool stuff. Cool stuff you will like. It learns about you and your tastes, then all you have to do is tap the StumbleUpon button and StumbleUpon will run off into the internet and instantly return with a whole bunch of stuff to float your boat, from pictures to videos to web pages. Believe it or not, this app will actually help you to get more out of the internet!

Akinator the Genie FREE

Price: Free
Developed By: Elokence
In-app Purchases: No

Think of any real or fictional character and, with just a few questions, the amazing Akinator the Genie will read your mind and tell you who you're thinking about. You can share your results on Facebook and the app has a child filter to let your children play safely. It sounds a bit daft, but it really is surprisingly clever and you'll find yourself scratching your head as it guesses you every time.

Plex

Price: £2.99
Developed By: Plex Inc
In-app Purchases: No

Plex is a great app that enables you to stream music, video and more from your home computer through your iPad or any other iOS device for that matter. You need to download the Plex software onto your computer first, and then follow the instructions to get it set up. This is a very cool piece of software and saves you having to store all your music and videos on your iPad, filling up all your storage space.

Justin.tv

Price: £2.99
Developed By: Justin.tv Inc
In-app Purchases: No

Justin.tv brings thousands of Internet video channels to your iPad for endless amounts of entertainment, with live events, foreign TV content, gaming events and more. Essentially, it's a little like YouTube, only broadcast live by individuals, companies, events or groups.

Of course, popular shows can have several thousand simultaneous viewers, which means the video quality will be down to the host's connection and the number of people viewing. Even so, Justin.tv can produce decent video-quality results thanks to peer-to-peer sharing.

The service is increasingly popular with video gamers to broadcast matches and indeed, computer users are one of the biggest groups on the service. If you're watching something notable, you can make comments and join in a chat about the show, or click the arrow button to share a channel with others or add it to your favourites.

While the Featured tab shows off the most popular content, the Categories tab offers Social, Entertainment, Gaming, Sports and News channels. You can watch all of these without the need to create an account, and it's free to do so.

Netflix

Price: Free
Developed By: Netflix, Inc.
In-app Purchases: Yes

Netflix is the world's leading subscription service for watching movies and TV episodes, and with this official Netflix app you can enjoy a world of entertainment anywhere, any time, with hundreds of movies and TV episodes available. If you are not yet a Netflix member, sign up when you install the app and start enjoying it immediately with a one-month free trial, followed by a cheap monthly subscription. The app includes full search features, or you can browse by category. Rate your favourites and Netflix will suggest new titles for you to watch.

Sky+

Price: Free
Developed By: BSkyB
In-app Purchases: No

The official Sky+ app is a great way to control your Sky+ HD box from your iPad. All you need to do is connect your Sky+ box to your broadband router. When your device is connected to the same network, it can act as a remote control to play, pause, fast-forward and rewind, or change channel. While you're out and about, you can view and search full seven-day programme listings, with highlights and recommendations, and remotely set your Sky+ box to record with Series Link, just as you would from home. Never miss any of your favourite shows again.

BlinkBox for iPad

Price: Free
Developed By: BlinkBox Entertainment
In-app Purchases: Yes (pay per view)

If you don't like the idea of signing up for a monthly subscription, then BlinkBox might be a good option for you. It's a movie streaming service that lets you rent or buy movies one at a time. Annoyingly, you can't actually buy things through this app; you'll need to do that on a PC, but once you've paid for your films, you'll be able to watch them on your iPad via the free app. There's a massive selection of films available, and new releases arrive promptly, so if there's something you fancy watching, it's worth seeing if it's on here. There's one catch – it only works over Wi-Fi.

iPad Air

Entertainment Apps (continued)

4oD Catch Up

Price: Free
Developed By: Channel 4
In-app Purchases: No

As probably the UK's edgiest terrestrial station, Channel 4's app has some of the sharpest comedy from Channel 4 and E4. It also has a catch-up feature (so you can watch all of a previously broadcast series in one sitting), guides to help you find the right show and parental controls if you want to let your children view something using the app.

ITV Player

Price: Free
Developed By: ITV
In-app Purchases: No

ITV's app has content from the four ITV stations plus CITV for children. Despite that, though, the whole thing seems a little content-light compared to other stations, focusing as it does on soaps and reality shows (if you like them, great). However, there are also some classic dramas like Sherlock Holmes, Inspector Morse and others.

Demand 5

Price: Free
Developed By: Channel 5
In-app Purchases: No

Channel 5's app has a host of Big Brother content accessible along with the last 30 days of other C5 shows to enjoy (if you can enjoy anything that Channel 5 puts on, that is). With impressive presentation, it's a good-looking app with plenty of content from the channel's many reality shows, Aussie soaps and documentaries to enjoy.

Sky Go

Price: Free (Subscription required)
Developed By: Sky
In-app Purchases: Yes (movies on demand)

Sky Go is an on-demand TV app that's mainly designed for Sky subscribers, but you can sign up for a monthly ticket on the Sky site to access Sky without a satellite dish. The app provides viewing for up to two devices per account, with the latest Sky movies, sports and TV shows available depending on the type of ticket you buy. It's also recently added Sky Atlantic.

Pictophile

Price: Free
Developed By: Voodoo Coding
In-app Purchases: No

If you've never seen a meme then the chances are you've never visited an internet forum. They're basically pictures with humorous captions, and Pictophile enables you to create your own memes in seconds. You can share and upload your own pictures or use other people's funny images and take advantage of several more cool features as well. If you like your memes, you'll love Pictophile.

Talking Tom & Ben News

Price: Free
Developed By: Out Fit 7 Ltd
In-app Purchases: Yes

If you haven't come across Tom and Ben before, they're a comical, cute dog and cat double act. You can say whatever you want into the microphone and Tom and Ben will repeat it back to you in their funny voices. It sounds silly, and it is, but it's also great fun and you can set up some pretty funny scenes using the additional interactive features. Gotta love talking animals!

Zeebox

Price: Free
Developed By: Zeebox
In-app Purchases: No

Zeebox brings social media and your TV viewing habits together in one app, in a way that it insists will revolutionise the way we watch TV. By that, we assume it means we'll spend all our time talking about the shows we're watching as we watch them, rather than just sitting down and enjoying them, and then talking about them afterwards. Anyway, you set it up by choosing your TV region and services (Virgin Media, Sky, BTVision and so on), and the app provides a guide to all the shows that are on.

Tap whichever one you're watching on the big screen and you can follow the streams from Twitter relating to that show on your iPad (which many TV channels have started promoting heavily both before and during shows), then talk with others and find out more about it, making this a powerful social tool for TV addicts.

Other tabs you can press include links to news and gossip about the show that you're watching while the Downloads tab shows apps, music, video or other related content that you can buy on iTunes, should you wish. Each show has a popularity meter, and as new hashtags about the show appear on Twitter, you can follow them, thereby monitoring the discussion about a particular character or event.

Tap the Activity tag to post your own comments to Twitter or to 'like' a show and if you have an Internet TV, you can even control that using the app.

X-Factor

Price: Free
Developed By: FremantleMedia Ltd
In-app Purchases: Yes

If you're a fan of the X-Factor (and judging by the viewing figures, most people are) then you're going to love this official companion app that comes packed with cool features. You can watch videos of your favourite performances, get profiles of the judges and the contestants and all the latest behind-the-scenes news and gossip. You can also play the Fifth Judge game and try to guess who will go through each week and ultimately win the competition. In short, this is an absolute must for X-Factor fans who can't get enough of the show.

Morfo

Price: Free
Developed By: SunSpark Labs
In-app Purchases: Yes

Morfo is such a cool app and you can have some real fun with it. It basically transforms face photos into 3D models. You can then apply make-up, silly effects, funny hairstyles and more. You can even make them sing and dance. The basic app is free, so you can try it out for nothing and if you like what you find, various additional effects packs can be purchased from within the app. It's throwaway fun for sure, but it's guaranteed to raise a smile. This is definitely one of our favourite 'silly' apps and a great way to make your friends do whatever you want!

Xbox One Smartglass

Price: Free
Developed By: Microsoft Corporation
In-app Purchases: No

These are exciting times for video gamers. The new generation of consoles has officially arrived. Smartglass for Xbox One is a remote control for your console that enables you to start it up and interact with it from your iPad, but it's more than that. It enables you to keep up with who's online, what they're up to, your achievements and more, even when you're away from the machine. It's a must for serious Xbox gamers. Just pay attention because there's a separate Smartglass app for the Xbox 360, so make sure you get the right one.

Your iPad Air and...
Music

Way, way back in 2001, Apple came along and completely revolutionised the way we listen to music when it launched the iPod. The iPad doesn't just enable you to listen to music though, nor does it merely let you carry your entire music collection around with you wherever you go. It also allows you to browse and buy new music through iTunes and download it direct to your iPad instantly. On top of that it's a recording studio. We've got a tutorial for GarageBand – Apple's own music studio app – which enables you to create, mix and produce your own music tracks with samples, drum loops and even real instruments. We also explain how iTunes works and how to buy music as well as how to rip your CDs and transfer them to your iPad via a computer.

The App Store is also home to thousands of innovative music apps, both serious and fun. We have a few recommendations for you to check out and if you enjoy music then you're sure to find something you'll like.

"GarageBand enables you to create, mix and produce your own music tracks with samples, drum loops and even real instruments"

62 How To Use iTunes

- Browse iTunes
- Hear A Track Preview
- Albums And Tracks
- Confirm Your Details
- Current Downloads
- Previous Purchases

How To Use... iTunes

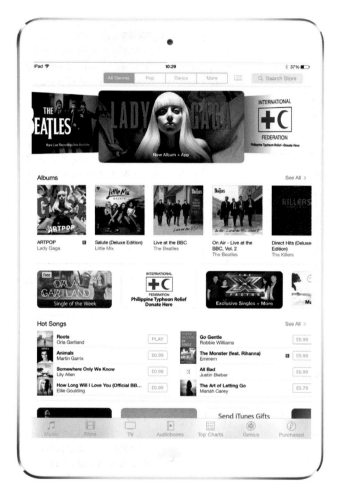

iTunes' huge library of music is available for download direct to your iPad. Here's how to browse and purchase albums and tracks from the world's largest and most popular music store.

Step 1: Browse iTunes

Thanks to the iTunes app that comes pre-loaded on the iPad, you can easily browse through the wide selection of music on offer by new releases, the latest charts, genre or what's hot right now. Alternatively, if you already know what you want, you can just search for an artist or song title via the Search Store field at the top of the screen.

Step 2: Hear A Track Preview

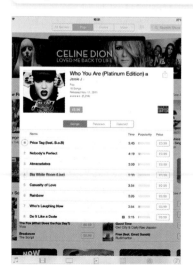

To hear a preview of any track in album view, click on the song number or name. It may take a short time to load up depending on your connection. Previews last 30 seconds and you can click the stop button to end it or on another track to preview that one, cancelling the first selection. If you're in a general view, you can double-tap a song to see the album it's from.

Step 3: Albums And Tracks

You'll notice that most songs have a price already marked next to them. Touch that price and you'll be able to download the song. Some songs, however, are only available as part of an album and not individually. If a song is listed as Album Only, you'll have to click the Buy Album button at the top of the page and buy the whole album to get the track you're after.

Step 4: Confirm Your Details

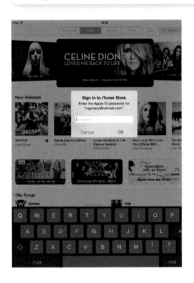

Usually, you'll be asked to enter your iTunes password to confirm a purchase. If a purchase fails, you'll need to go to Settings, then tap Store Apple ID, View Apple ID and then Payment Information to check your card details. Once a purchase is confirmed, active downloads will be highlighted with a number indicating how many songs are still to be downloaded.

Step 5: Current Downloads

If you have a number of songs downloading, you can follow their progress on the Downloads screen. A number shows how many files are still to download and you can tap to see the file sizes and download progress of each one. You can't play songs through the iTunes app though; you have to open Music to play your downloaded tracks once transfer is complete.

Step 6: Previous Purchases

If you've downloaded music to a computer or another iOS device linked to your Apple ID, you can tap the Purchased option at the bottom of the page and choose Recent Purchases to find those songs listed there. Tap Download All Songs to copy every file in the list to your iPad or just tap the button next to a song to download individual tracks instead.

How To... Transfer CDs To Your iPad Air

iTunes enables you to buy and download music directly to your iPad, but what about your CD collection.
This tutorial explains how to rip your CDs to your computer using iTunes and then copy them to your iPad.

Step 1: Getting Started

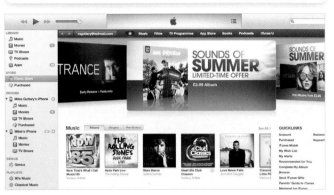

Firstly, you need to put a music CD into your computer. If you're using a Mac, iTunes will open automatically. On a PC, you should choose the option Import Songs Using iTunes. If this is not offered, you can open iTunes manually from the start menu or by right clicking on the CD drive and choosing Open With and iTunes.

Step 2: Choosing Tracks To Import

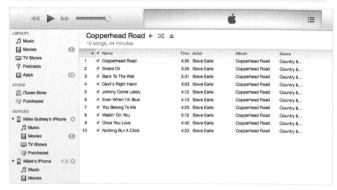

When iTunes is open it will automatically find the track details for your CD. Check these are correct (because there are some errors in the database). All the tracks will be selected at first, if there are any that you don't want to import, you can deselect them by clicking on the box next to the track number on the left hand side.

Step 3: Changing The Import Format

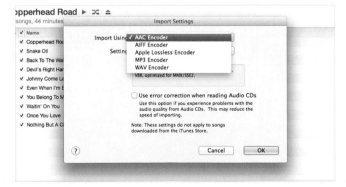

When you click on Import Settings, you have the option to change the data encoder as different devices recognise different file types. Almost any device will be able to play MP3 files, while your iPad can recognise either MP3 or AAC files, so one of these will be the best option for you when importing files.

Step 4: Changing The Audio Quality

Also under the Import Settings menu it is possible to determine the audio quality of the files you import. Quality is measured in kbps (kilobytes per second) and the higher this figure, the better the quality, but be aware that higher quality files take up more memory. If you need a more detailed explanation, click on the Help button.

iTip – ALBUM COVERS
When you've imported a CD, hold CTRL and click on the blank album icon. You'll see the option Get Album Artwork. Select it and iTunes will attempt to find it for you.

Step 5: Importing Your Music Tracks

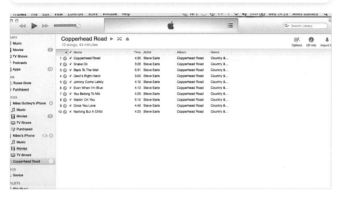

When you're satisfied that you have chosen the correct format for your music, all you have to do is click the Import CD button. It should take about 30 seconds for each track to complete; a green tick will appear next to the track number when it has finished. You can stop the process at any time by pressing the Stop Importing button.

Step 6: Connect To Your Computer

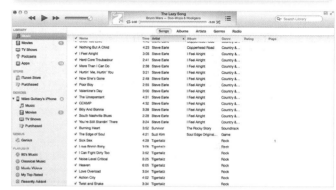

Now you need to put the imported tracks on to your iPad, so connect it to your computer with the USB lead. iTunes will detect that the iPad is connected and your it will appear in the left pane. Click on it to check you have enough free space, you may have to wait a moment while the iPad syncs up.

Step 7: Copying Over Your Music

To choose what you want to copy you must first click on the Music tab at the top of the screen. Here you can choose Sync Music to copy either your entire music library or particular playlists/albums/artists/genres. If you want to copy a selection of individual tracks, just drag them onto your iPad manually.

Step 8: Finishing And Playing

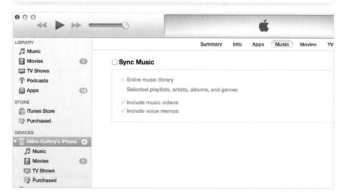

When your tracks have finished copying, disconnect your iPad properly by first pressing the eject button next to the icon. To listen to your music, all you need to do is open the Music App and tap the track or album you want to hear. The only drawback is the process can take a long time if you have a lot of CDs.

GarageBand

Price: £2.99
Developed By: Apple
In-App Purchases: No

If you're interested in any kind of music recording then you'll definitely want to check out GarageBand. It's a music studio you can carry with you in your pocket and with a bit of practice you can create professional-sounding tracks.

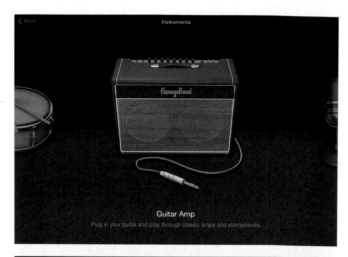

Guitar Amp
Plug in your guitar and play through classic amps and stompboxes.

Although it doesn't have the screen space, system memory or storage capacity that you'd normally expect from a serious music creation app, GarageBand for iPad manages to cram a heck of a lot of creative possibilities into a small space. The fact that Apple is only charging £2.99 for it is pretty remarkable too given that the full desktop version is part of the iLife suite that comes in at around £40. Of course, the low price doesn't mean it's a small app. The download is a hefty 500MB, so it will take up a fair chunk of your storage.

At its simplest, GarageBand enables you to pick instruments from a selection of drums, keyboards, guitars, basses and more, play around with them for a bit until you work out a tune or even just a few notes and then lay something down. You can record anything you create on the eight-track sequencer provided and then add further instruments or samples to create a complete track. While it's small and easy to use, don't underestimate the capacity of the app to create a serious piece of music. For amateurs, various levels of autoplay mean the app can help you to create a pleasant sounding tune by maintaining timing and key, while an extensive range of synthesizers and effects mean that with practice and experimentation you should be able to achieve the sound you want.

Once you've experimented with the various basic instruments, you'll find that the guitars can play in chord or note mode across a range of scales, while the blues and electric guitars have a number of pedals that you can use to alter their sound. Once you've found a sound you like, you can really get to work.

When you've perfected a tune, you can then record it, move into the eight-track sequencer and use it as the basis for a full song using short bursts of samples or audio recordings to go along with the instrumentals.

Unfortunately you can't plug in a keyboard, but you can connect a guitar through the earphone socket to record some real strings.

GarageBand on iPad can also be used to import a range of existing samples, enabling you to create on the go. There are some samples stored in the app, but musicians will likely have their own they'll want to use, and the usual formats including Apple Loops, AIFF, WAV, CAF, AAC and MP3 files are all compatible. Music can be exported in data or song form to be edited on another device if you ever need or want to do so.

With just a little effort and no real musical skill, it's possible to use GarageBand to create a great sounding tune that you can play on your iPad and share with friends. However, it does have plenty to offer the serious musician as well. If you have any interest in creating music then GarageBand is most definitely for you.

iPad Air

How To Use... GarageBand

GarageBand is a very flexible app that gives you a lot of scope for creating your own tracks.
The following steps will get you started with the basics and from there the world of music is your oyster.

Step 1: Picking An Instrument

The first thing to do when you start GarageBand is to pick
an instrument. You can choose from Smart Keyboard,
Smart Guitar, Smart Bass or a basic keyboard and drum
kit. Scroll horizontally to make your choice, it's probably
best to start with Smart Keyboard for the moment and get
straight down to making some music.

Step 2: Changing The Keyboard Settings

Each instrument has a variety of settings controlling the
sound and how it's produced; hit the sliders icon to bring
up the settings menu. As well as volume, pan, echo and
reverb, there are options for quantisation and transposition
(to make sure it's in the correct time and key) and velocity
(controlling how sensitive it is to your touch).

Step 3: Setting Autoplay

If you have selected a smart instrument, you'll notice
there is an autoplay facility. On the lowest setting this will
produce a basic chord pattern for you to play along with;
the higher you set the dial, the more complex the track
will get. This backing track will be recorded along with
whatever you play.

Step 4: The Smart Keyboard

When you have autoplay activated, the Smart Keyboard
makes things very simple, hit any key and it will
automatically play in time, or tap one from the top and one
from the bottom and they will both play. Mess around for
a little while and see what it can do, and when you think
you've hit on something worth recording read on...

iPad Air

How To Use... GarageBand (continued)

Step 5: Recording Your First Track

When you're ready to start recording, hit the red circle button at the top to begin. You can keep recording for as long you like. Parts you don't like can always be cut out later, but when you're ready to move on, tap the stop button. Now let's go to the sequencer screen; the sequencer icon is the second one from the left.

Step 6: Using The Eight-Track Sequencer

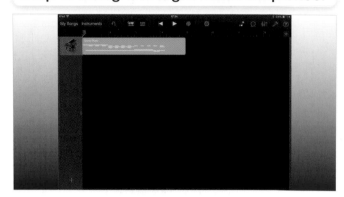

Here you can see a visible representation of what you have just recorded. Tap the play button to listen back, if it's no good, you can always delete it and start again. If, however, you are satisfied with your work, you can now add another instrument; touch the plus sign and you will be taken back to the main screen.

Step 7: Playing The Smart Guitar

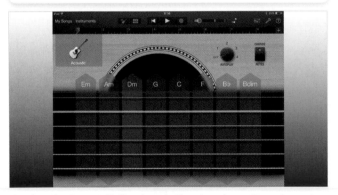

To play the Smart Guitar, touch the chords on the relevant strings to produce a sound, the Basic Guitar gives you more options such as bending strings to produce different effects. Again, just play around to see how it works. Repeat steps 3 to 6 as above to get something recorded that you can put in your finished song.

Step 8: Adding A Drum Track

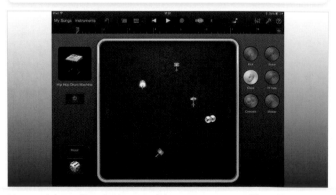

Now add another instrument to your composition. Tap Instruments and choose Smart Drums from the options. You don't have the choice of autoplay with drums, so you're on your own; place the drum sounds into the box in the middle of the screen or choose random (dice icon) and see what happens, then record the same way as above.

Step 9: Testing And Adding Samples

From the sequencer, you can access audio samples from the loop icon at the top. Go to Apple Loops and browse the samples until something takes your fancy, add it to your project by holding your finger down on the icon to the left of the name and dragging it into an empty track in the sequencer when it pops up.

Step 10: Working In The Sequencer

To get a good sounding track, you need to make sure each element is playing at the right volume; drag open the instrument panel on the left to reveal the volume options. This will allow you to bring each track up or down in the mix, or to mute it completely. To get rid of the volume controls, flick it back to the left.

Step 11: Moving And Shortening Tracks

In the sequencer, you can trim down any tracks that have superfluous elements by dragging the start or end points inwards to cut out bits you don't like. You can reposition any track within your composition by dragging it backwards or forwards, you can also delete or duplicate it by touching it and choosing the appropriate option.

Step 12: Outputting Your Track

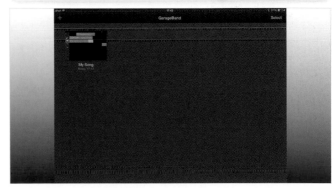

When you quit GarageBand, it will save the project you were working on automatically. To see all your works, tap where it says My Songs in the top left hand corner and all your recorded tracks will appear. If you want to share what you've created with your friends, you can do it from here, and you can also send it to iTunes if you like.

iPad Air

Music Apps

If you're a musician or just a music fan, there are hundreds of apps for the iPad that will help you to listen to, play and compose your own tunes and more. Here are a few of our favourites for you to take a look at.

Spotify

Price: Free
Developed By: Spotify Ltd
In-app Purchases: Yes

Want a massive music collection without having to download it onto your iPad? Then Spotify is the answer. It allows you to take over 15 million songs on the go with both streaming and offline modes – you need to subscribe once the free trial is over, but it's well worth it for an inexhaustible source of both new and familiar tunes.

Guitar!

Price: Free
Developed By: On Beat Limited
In-app Purchases: Yes

There are a lot of guitar apps in the App Store, but this is one of the best. Featuring professionally-recorded high-quality samples from a Cole Clark FL3 guitar, this is about as close as you'll ever get to actually playing a guitar on your iPad. It features hundreds of chords, with the fret board and a recording feature as in-app purchases.

Songsterr Guitar Tabs

Price: £6.99
Developed By: Guitar Tabs LLC
In-app Purchases: No

Tablature, or "tab", is a type of written music specifically for guitar, bass and drums. This feature-packed, top-rated app has over half a million tabs for guitar and bass, as well as chords and drum tabs. The app may seem expensive, but it includes royalty payments to the musicians who wrote the songs, so it's all fully licensed.

Cleartune Chromatic Tuner

Price: £2.49
Developed By: bitcount
In-app Purchases: No

If you play guitar or bass you'll need a tuner, and they don't come much better than Cleartune. It features a high-quality fine-tunable chromatic tuner and pitch pipe that can be used to tune almost any instrument, as well as support for custom tunings, transposition, odd notations and lots more. An invaluable tool for musicians.

FourChords HD

Price: Free
Developed By: Musopia
In-app Purchases: No

Four Chords Guitar Karaoke is a great way to learn new songs on your guitar. It uses a simple karaoke-style display that shows you the chords to play and song lyrics, and accompanies you with a backing track. Songs have been specially arranged to be easy to play, and no knowledge of tabs or sheet music is required, just the ability to play those four magic chords.

rad.io

Price: Free
Developed By: radio.de GmbH
In-app Purchases: Yes

With this app you can listen to your choice of over 7,000 radio stations from around the world, as well as local stations from your region. Search for stations by categories including genre, topic, city and country, or follow editorial recommendations. Save stations as favourites and automatically find similar stations. The perfect app for radioheads of the world.

djay 2

Price: £2.99
Developed By: algoriddim
In-app Purchases: No

This is the second generation of the world's best-selling DJ app for iOS devices, a winner of the Apple Design Award, and it's been entirely redesigned to make it even better. With djay your iOS device becomes a fully featured DJ system with virtual decks, and your tunes are turned into virtual records complete with accurately modelled grooves, so that you can see where the breaks are, just like a real vinyl disk. Mix and scratch your music on a realistic turntable interface with direct access to all your favourite songs and playlists.

You can perform live, record mixes wherever you are, or use the Automix mode to let djay create mixes for you automatically. Whether you're a professional DJ or a beginner who just loves to play music, djay 2 offers you the most intuitive and powerful DJ experience you'll find on iOS.

Version 2 includes a huge list of new features, far too many to go into here, but highlights include a new user interface, sampler and drum pads, a new music library, advanced performance tools and HD Waveforms to help you visualise your music. This is one of the best music apps available, and a bargain at the price.

Groovy Beats

Price: Free
Developed By: TapMafia LLC
In-app Purchases: Yes

This smart little app lets you create music quickly and easily by tapping out patterns on your screen. It's so easy to use that it's ideal for teaching kids about music. With two instruments in the free version and eight more as in-app purchases (or all ten if you buy the paid version) there's plenty of variety available. Each instrument has its own volume control, and you can use each as often as you like. You can upload your musical compositions to Facebook or Soundcloud so your friends can rate them. It makes even the non-musical musical.

Shazam

Price: Free
Developed By: Shazam Entertainment Ltd
In-app Purchases: Yes

The miraculous Shazam has been available for a while now, but if you're unfamiliar with it, it can identify (almost) any piece of music you hear. Just start up the app, let it hear a snippet of a song and within moments it will tell you everything you want to know, from the name of the song to who recorded it. Other similar apps are available but Shazam is the original and, for us, the best. If you've ever heard a song you've liked and wondered what it was but weren't able to find out, you know how frustrating that can be, but not with Shazam.

Tiny Piano

Price: Free
Developed By: squarepoet, inc.
In-app Purchases: Yes

If you've ever wanted to play the piano but don't have the time or patience for music lessons, help may be at hand in the shape of Tiny Piano. It lets you play tunes by tapping the screen of your device – sort of. In fact your taps only control the tempo – the notes that you play are in a pre-recorded sequence. You get 95 songs included in the free version, with a further seven song packs available as in-app purchases. Alternatively, there's a pro version with all the songs included. A popular and fun app that's guaranteed to amuse all the family.

Your iPad Air And
Games

The iPad is terrific gaming device and the App Store is packed with games in every genre you can think of. In this section we've got reviews of some of the coolest games available, but this selection represents just a tiny fraction of what's on offer. The great thing about iPad games is that most only cost a few pence and many are completely free. If you're unsure about how to buy and download a game, don't worry. We have a tutorial that explains everything you need to know. We've also got a tutorial that explains how to use Game Center. This fantastic feature enables you to compete with players from all over the world and see how your scores stack up. You can also make new friends and earn achievements. Confused? Check out pages 76-77 and everything will instantly become clear. Happy gaming!

"The great thing about iPad games is that most only cost a few pence and many are completely free"

74 How To Download games

- Games In The App Store
- Games By Category
- Searching For Games
- Ratings And Reviews
- Buy And Install Games
- Finding Your Games

76 How To Use Game Center

- What Is Game Center?
- The Interface
- Games
- Leaderboards
- Find New Friends
- See Your Achievements

78 Games

- XCOM: Enemy Unknown
- Bridge Constructor
- Six-Guns
- Temple Run
- Sonic The Hedgehog
- Bad Piggies HD
- Star Wars Pinball 2
- GTA: Vice City
- Hungry Shark Evolution
- Plants Vs Zombies
- Plague Inc
- Zombieville USA 2
- Angry Birds Star Wars HD
- Asphalt 7: Heat
- Cut The Rope
- Minecraft Pocket Edition
- Infinity Blade II
- Where's My Water
- Fruit Ninja
- Broken Sword: DC
- Jurassic Park Builder
- Modern Combat 3
- Dead Trigger
- Football Manager Handheld
- Campus Life
- Hero Academy
- Symphonica
- Words With Friends HD
- Tiny Tower
- Metal Slug 1
- Incoboto
- SongPop
- Radballs
- Magnetic Billiards: Blueprint
- Coaster Crazy
- Bumpy Road
- Agent Dash
- Burnout CRASH!

How To... Download games

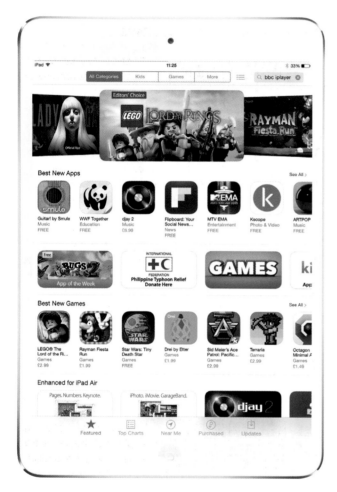

The iPad is a powerful games machine with a huge library of games in every genre you can think of. Unlock the awesome gaming potential with this simple tutorial.

Step 1: Games In The App Store

Your first port of call will be the App Store app. Tap the icon and you'll be magically transported to a tempting shop front of assorted goodies. The home page includes carousels of featured games that change each day. Here you'll be able to see all the latest big releases, recommendations and most popular games of the moment. Browse around and check it out.

Step 2: Games By Category

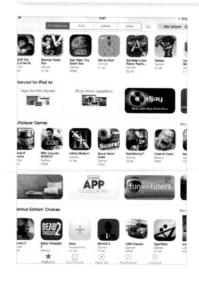

Along the top of the screen on the home page you'll see a tool bar with four options – All Categories, Kids, Games and More. Tap Games and you'll see a drop down menu that lists a comprehensive selection of game genres. Simply select the one you fancy and you'll see a new selection of carousels under the headings New, What's Hot, Paid and Free.

Step 3: Searching For Games

If you can't find the particular game you're looking for, fear not. The search field in the top right-hand corner enables you to hunt for it by title or keyword. Don't worry about getting the title of the game absolutely spot-on, because the search bar will helpfully provide you with a drop down list of results as you type. If you see the game you want appear, just tap its name.

Step 4: Ratings And Reviews

Once you've narrowed down your search to the game you want, click on it. A smaller screen will appear where you can see further details and ratings and read reviews. If the game is expensive it's worth checking out the reviews but keep in mind there are a lot of very moany people out there who are quite happy to dish out one-star ratings for little good reason!

Step 5: Buy And Install Games

When you're ready to buy the game, click on the price and it will prompt you to enter your Apple ID. You'll then see it start to download. A circular bar shows you the progress of the download. You'll also receive an email receipt to the email address associated with your Apple ID from Apple confirming the transaction has been made.

Step 6: Finding Your Games

Give it a few minutes to install and then you'll be able to start playing. You'll find the game app in the nearest available slot on the home screen. You may have to swipe a few screens to find it. Just tap it to enjoy the iPad gaming experience! You'll find these game apps are a brilliant way of killing time and your iPad will be filled with dozens of the things within days, we guarantee it!

How To Use... Game Center

Most games you download from the App Store feature Game Center connectivity, enabling you to meet and challenge other iOS gamers from around the world at your favourite games.

Step 1: What Is Game Center?

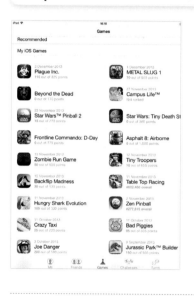

Game Center is the place where all your scores and achievements are recorded in all the games you play. You'll find the app on the home screen. If you're signed in with your Apple ID then Game Center should be ready to go. Just tap on it to open it and the first thing you'll see is the floaty bubble interface (it looks very different from the old version).

Step 2: The Interface

The interface basically appears twice on the main Game Center Screen. The functions of the bubbles (other than requests) are replicated by the more traditional tab navigation controls at the bottom of the screen. Each one is pretty self-explanatory. Tap them to go to the corresponding part of the app or tap Me at the bottom left to return to the main Game Center screen at any time.

Step 3: Games

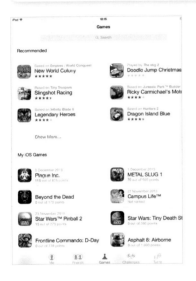

The Games tab is the part you're going to be most interested in. Tap on this to see a list of all the games you own or have played. You'll also see recommendations of games you might like to try out. These are based on the games that you've previously downloaded and also games that your friends are playing. You can tap these to go directly to the App Store and buy them right away.

Step 4: Leaderboards

The best thing about Game Center is that it enables you to see where you stack up against your friends and the rest of the world. To see the leaderboard for a particular game, select it from the list. There may be multiple leaderboards available, so select the one you want and see where you rank in the wide world of iOS gaming. You can also choose to 'like' a game if you wish.

Step 5: Find New Friends

You can add and search for friends in the Friends section. You'll also get recommendations of people you might like to befriend based on the games you and they have been playing. Tap on a friend's name to see their friends, how many Game Center points they've amassed and what games they've been playing. You can also challenge them at a game to show them who's top dog.

Step 6: See Your Achievements

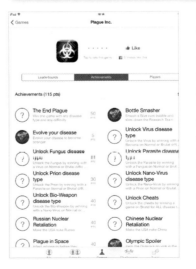

Every game has achievements. These are awards you receive for accomplishing certain goals in the game. To see your achievements for any game, tap on the game title then tap the Achievements tab. If you delete a game from your iPad you'll get the option to delete all Game Center stats associated with it, or you can keep them in case you decide to download it again.

iPad Air

77

Your iPad Air And Gaming

XCOM: Enemy Unknown

Price: £13.99
Developed By: 2K Games
In-app Purchases: No

When you charge this much for an iOS game, it had better be good. Well, fear not – this is one of the deepest, most compelling and addictive games you'll play in a long time.

Above: Take command of a top secret global initiative and defeat inter-galactic invaders in this modern strategy classic

Youngsters may not have heard of XCOM, but if you were a gamer in the 1990s then you're almost certain to have come across this classic of the strategy genre. Its roots can be traced right back to the early 1980s and the innovative work of game designer Julian Gollop. The influence of his early titles, which culminated in the turn-based classic Laser Squad released in 1988, is still very evident here.

The game places you in command of XCOM, a secret military initiative set up to combat the threat of alien invasion and it's up to you to keep the world safe. To do so you need to establish and build a base, set up a worldwide scanning network, position interceptors and micromanage the whole intricate operation.

Your base itself acts as the hub of the game. It contains different facilities such as research labs and manufacturing areas. You need to research alien artefacts recovered from missions and you can then use this knowledge to construct new weapons. Everything costs money though, and this is earned by completing missions and earning funding from different nations. Be careful though, if you don't protect countries they may pull their funding, making life very difficult for you.

The meat of the gameplay is turn-based strategy. Every time a UFO is shot down or an alien encounter is reported, you need to despatch a team to check out the situation and deal with the threat. The gameplay is very simple, but the strategy complex. Careful positioning of troops is vital each turn to ensure you don't get snuck up on. Keeping your guys alive is important as they level up with experience and you'll need your skilled veterans when it comes to the later missions. Troops can be trained in different skills from snipers to assault specialists and you'll need to select the right mix for each mission. There really is so much depth to the strategy, which you might not appreciate at first.

The one thing that might have surprised you is the price of the game. Obviously it's hugely expensive compared to other

iOS games, but this is a perfect conversion of a game that came out as a full price home console release less than two years ago. There's no difference between this and the Xbox 360/PlayStation 3 game.

If strategy isn't your bag then you might want to give it a miss. This is a slow-paced game that rewards patience, thought and experience. If you've played any of the XCOM games, or the likes of Lords of Chaos, Laser Squad and Rebelstar from the 80s, then you're going to love Enemy Unknown. Don't be put off by the price, you'll be playing this for months. It combines a cool story with resource management and seamlessly blends it with action strategy. The action itself takes on an extra dimension thanks to the importance of keeping your troops alive and you truly develop an emotional connection with them as they progress through their careers. It's always a sad moment when a soldier who's been with you for a long time doesn't make it, and not many games manage to achieve that. This is a modern classic.

Bridge Constructor

Price: £1.49
Developed By: Headup Games GmbH & Co KG
In-app Purchases: Yes

Above: Red indicates dangerous levels of stress on the structure. This bridge design needs some serious reconsideration

It's always good to see an original take on a familiar theme and Bridge Constructor offers exactly that. As the title implies, this game is all about building bridges. Essentially it's a physics-based puzzle game that requires you to use a combination of common sense, trial-and-error and occasional outside-the-box thinking in order to construct bridges that span various chasms and rivers. For each bridge, you're given a limited amount of resources and a cash budget. Each unit of a resource costs money and the idea is to create a stable bridge using girders, towers and suspension cables. The most stable sections of the bridge appear green, while sections that glow red are under extreme stress and may give way. The acid test comes when you're happy with your construction and it hasn't already collapsed under it's own weight. First you'll want to drive a

couple of cars across it and, if it survives that, the ultimate test is lorries. If your bridge can support these, then it can support anything.

Things get pretty tough pretty quickly. With larger spans to cross and new materials being made available as you progress, it constantly throws new challenges at you. With plenty of levels to tackle this is a highly original game that'll keep you going for a long, long time.

Six-Guns

Price: Free
Developed By: Gameloft
In-app Purchases: No

This is a bit of an oddity. It starts out as though it's going to be a sandbox style spaghetti western in the vein of Red Dead Redemption, but quickly takes a turn for the bizarre with zombies, monsters and crazy new weapons all showing up against the wild west backdrop. If an authentic western is what you're looking for, then this isn't it, but it's an extremely fun third person shooter with some nice visuals that keeps the surprises coming thick and fast. Its also free, and you can't really say fairer than that. Now, how about a serious western?

Temple Run

Price: Free
Developed By: Imangi Studios
In-app Purchases: No

This is one of those games that defines the concept of less is more. Visually it looks sharp with fast moving 3D graphics, but the gameplay is nothing more than a series of well-timed swipes and taps. Your character must run at top speed, avoiding all manner of nasty pitfalls, and it's up to you to ensure he doesn't come to a sticky end. Several versions of Temple Run are available on the App Store but the concept always remains the same and we have a particularly soft spot for the original.

Sonic The Hedgehog

Price: £0.99
Developed By: SEGA of America
In-app Purchases: No

Sonic the Hedgehog is a legend. His enduring popularity is a testament to the quality of the early Sonic games. Lesser reputations might have been crushed under the weight of all the sub-par Sonic titles that have come out since. This is the original though, and this is Sonic how he should be. It's fast, it's brash and it's skilful. You've played it a thousand times before, but like all the best games, one more go always seems like a good idea, and it remains as playable today as it was 20 years ago.

Bad Piggies HD

Price: Free
Developed By: Rovio Mobile Ltd
In-app Purchases: No

Spin-offs of big franchises are rarely anything to write home about, but Rovio have certainly bucked that particular trend with this superb off-shoot of the Angry Birds series.

If you've any interest in gaming or popular culture then you'll know about Angry Birds. It's one of the most simplistic games imaginable and yet it's swept the world. Later iterations like Angry Birds Space and Angry Birds Star Wars added much needed skill and variety to the mix, but nothing on the scale of Bad Piggies.

If you're not up to speed on the whole Angry Birds thing, the reason they're so angry is that a bunch of pigs keep stealing their eggs. Up to now the whole story has been played out from the birds' point of view and the poor piggies have been nothing more than cannon fodder for a worldwide barrage of feathery missiles. Well not any more! The piggies have got a game all of their very own and it's one of the funniest, most original and inventive puzzle games around.

Like Angry Birds, each level is a side view 2D cartoon landscape, but there the similarity ends. The aim is to get your pig to the finish point through the construction of bizarre and hare-brained contraptions. They start off simple enough, but as you reach the later levels they can become huge, complex feats of engineering.

The game's learning curve is perfectly pitched, gradually introducing one or two new elements each level. At first a couple of boxes and a set of wheels will be enough to get you from A to B. Fast forward a few levels and you'll find yourself working umbrella parachutes, helium balloons, engines, nitro boosts and various other gubbins into your designs. It's incredibly satisfying when a particularly loopy looking machine actually manages to accomplish the task at hand, but it's almost as amusing to witness the many spectacular failures that you'll experience along the way. It can be hilarious when things backfire or don't quite work in the way you expected them to.

The game's split into ground and flying levels, each of which give you various materials and components to mess around with. Like Angry Birds, you earn a star rating for each level. Three challenges must be completed on the

way to reaching the finish line to earn all three stars. These challenges could be to collect items, get to the end within a time limit or not use a particular component. Stars in turn open up sandbox levels. These are huge, open levels where you can play about with contraption designs to your heart's content. Progress through the main game earns you more components to use in the sandbox levels which provides a nice synergy between the two elements.

Bad Piggies is a masterpiece of originality, game design and presentation. The sound effects deserve special mention as they compliment the game perfectly and add to the hilarity no end. At times it's like an interactive Looney Tunes cartoon. Best of all, because it uses Rovio's well tested physics routines, you'll never see exactly the same crash twice. Bad Piggies is just an awesome game from front to back.

Star Wars Pinball 2

Price: £1.49
Developed By: ZEN Studios Ltd
In-app Purchases: Yes

They'll put the Star Wars name to anything these days, and if you're a fan you'd be forgiven for uttering a sigh when you hear the words Star Wars and pinball together. Before you go and find a corner to sob in, you should know that this is excellent, nay, brilliant, nay – the best pinball game on the iPad by far! You only get one table for your money (more are available via in-app purchase), but it's so good it doesn't matter. The polish and effort that's gone into the game is clearly evident. The table is feature-packed, the movement physics are spot on and the game is packed with memorable quotes and cool animations when you activate certain features and bonuses. Anyone can pick it up and play, but getting the big scores takes skill and practice.

It's simple. If you love pinball, you'll love this. If you love Star Wars and pinball then you'll love this like a son. Few games can boast this level of just-one-more-go-ability and you'll find yourself actually wishing bus journeys would take a little longer. Once you get into it you'll almost certainly want to purchase the additional tables as well, it's that good.

GTA: Vice City

Price: £2.99
Developed By: Rockstar Games
In-app Purchases: No

Grand Theft Auto III pioneered open world, urban sandbox-style gaming, but the majority of fans agree that the sequel, Vice City, was actually a superior game. You can now revisit this amazing game, perfectly recreated for mobile devices. In fact, thanks to its HD makeover, it actually looks better than the original. If you remember the game from the first time around, you know what it's all about; if you missed out on this gem then now's your chance to catch up and get acquainted with a true classic.

Hungry Shark Evolution

Price: Free
Developed By: Future Games of London
In-app Purchases: Yes

We've all seen Jaws and been scared of the big, bad shark, right? But have you ever tried to see the movie from the shark's point of view? He's just trying to make his way through life in the way sharks do, the poor chap. Now you can experience shark life for yourself with the awesomely fun Hungry Shark. The concept is simple – you're a shark and you need to eat. That means fish, crabs, scuba divers, swimmers; they're all fair game. Eat, stay alive and unlock bigger, hungrier sharks. What more could you possibly want in a game?

Plants Vs Zombies

Price: £0.69
Developed By: EA Swiss Sarl
In-app Purchases: Yes

What happens when tower defence, horticulture and the undead collide? Plants Vs Zombies, that's what. Grow more and more powerful defensive vegetation in your garden to drive back increasingly aggressive waves of zombies determined to eat your brain. This game is as addictive and playable as it is ridiculous. Brilliant cartoon graphics and a heavy helping of humour in the zombie descriptions make this one of the most fun games available on any format. If you've never experienced Plants Vs Zombies before, you need to let it into your life.

Your iPad Air And Gaming

Plague Inc

Price: Free
Developed By: Ndemic Creations
In-app Purchases: Yes

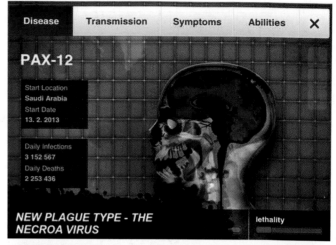

NEW PLAGUE TYPE - THE NECROA VIRUS

RELEASE A PLAGUE ACROSS THE GLOBE

Have you ever wondered what it would be like to be a teeny tiny microbe blowing on the breeze? If the answer is yes then, quite frankly, you must be a little bit weird.

In the vast majority of games that put the human race in danger, you're the one tasked with the job of saving the day. In Plague Inc your ultimate goal is to wipe out the whole of humanity. So what are you? A crazed super villain? An evil megalomaniacal despot? Nope and nope, you're a microbe, a nasty little germ that, at the start of the game, nobody cares about. But they will. Oh yes. They will!

After you choose a difficulty setting, you get to choose what type of disease you want to be from various options, more of which are unlocked each time you complete the game with a different one.

You're then presented with the main game screen, which is a world map, and the first decision you have to make is where to locate the first outbreak of your disease. This is a big strategic decision, the impact of which will be felt later on. An obvious starting point is an African country; not only is it easy for your disease to spread across the continent's land borders, quickly infecting millions, but with many underdeveloped nations, they will struggle to come up with an effective cure. However, once the spread of your disease is noticed by major countries, they will start pouring more and more resources into coming up with a cure. For this reason, you might want to start your outbreak in Europe or the United States. The initial spread may not be as rapid, but in the longer run this may hamper humanity's efforts to find a cure. As the game progresses you can access all sorts of data including death rates, percentage of the population that has been infected and progress towards development of an effective cure.

Once significant numbers of people start becoming infected, people will start serious research into a cure and this is where the real battle begins. As your outbreak becomes more serious, you earn points which can be spent on mutations that have very different effects. Some make your disease more resistant to medical treatments, others enable different methods of contagion. You can also dramatically increase the fatality rate of your disease, but it's a balancing act; the more people that die, the more aggressively people

will work towards a cure. You could try to create the deadliest disease possible and hope to wipe out the population before they have a chance to act, or you could go more covert, keeping the death rate down while you maximise infection and then introduce deadlier mutations later in the cycle.

The goal is to wipe out every single human being. If the cure is completed, you'll have to start over and rethink your methods. It's the tactical cat and mouse that makes Plague Inc so compulsive. With so many elements to consider and so many possible approaches, you'll come back to it again and again. The highest difficulty setting provides a really stern challenge that you won't beat without putting some serious time in. When you do, new diseases are unlocked.

It's the interesting concept of Plague Inc that will first attract people, but the simple gameplay and strategic depth will keep you coming back. This is without doubt one of the best and most original mobile games around.

Zombieville USA 2

Price: £0.69
Developed By: Mika Mobile Inc
In-app Purchases: No

You're probably sighing at the thought of yet another zombie game, but if they're of the quality of this and Plants Vs Zombies then keep 'em coming, we say! Zombieville USA 2 harks back to the golden age of arcade gaming. You walk left to right, hosing anything that ventures onto the screen with bullets. Rather than reaching the end of a stage, the goal is to stay alive long enough to be picked up by a rescue helicopter. Increasingly tough stages make this harder and harder, which is why you need bigger guns. It's the huge range of customisable weapons that keep you coming back to this game. There's always something new to save up for and try out. Every weapon has five levels of upgrades and you can also buy and upgrade special abilities for your character. It can be a bit of a grind to get these as it takes quite a long time to earn money, but you'll be having

so much fun doing it, so who cares? You can even play co-op over Wi-Fi, which is crazy good fun. Brilliant graphics and airtight controls make this a perfect game to blow off steam with. You can play it for a few minutes whenever you find yourself at a loose end, and everything you do earns a few more coins towards that next awesome upgrade.

Angry Birds Star Wars HD

Price: £1.99
Developed By: Rovio Mobile Ltd
In-app Purchases: No

The wild success of Angry Birds was based on a very basic physics-based exercise in trial and error. The fact that it became one of the biggest success stories in entertainment made it seem a perfect bedfellow for the Star Wars franchise, at least in terms of marketing and merchandising overkill. Surprisingly though, this marriage of seemingly unmeshable licences turned out to be the best Angry Birds game yet, with various Star Wars elements adding a whole new layer of skill to the gameplay. Take our word for it, it rocks. Honest!

Asphalt 7: Heat

Price: £0.69
Developed By: Gameloft
In-app Purchases: No

Asphalt 7 is the seventh game in the acclaimed Asphalt mobile racing series. After seven games you'd imagine the developers would have things pretty much down, and you'd be right. This is a blindingly fast arcade-style racer in which the idea is to go very, very fast and hopefully make it safely round the next bend and then the one after that. Finding shortcuts, grabbing collectibles and setting unbeatable times are the main aims. Finely tuned gameplay, great graphics and tight controls make it a blast.

Cut The Rope

Price: £0.69
Developed By: Zepto La
In-app Purchases: No

Cut The Rope is one of the most fun, original and enduringly popular puzzle games on mobile formats. The physics-based puzzles involve the player cutting ropes at the right time and in the correct sequence to feed the cute monster Om Nom. It starts off easy but, as with the best puzzlers, it soon becomes fiendishly tricky. First working out what you have to do and then successfully managing to pull it off are as satisfying as can be and the cute graphics never get boring to look at. This is everything a puzzler should be.

Your iPad Air And Gaming

Minecraft Pocket Edition

Price: £4.99
Developed By: Mojang
In-app Purchases: No

The amazing Minecraft comes to mobile devices and it's just as wildly addictive as ever it was. It's not as feature-heavy as the PC version, but that's to be expected and it still has that uncanny knack of consuming hours of your life without you even noticing. If you haven't heard of it before, basically it involves digging, building and creating your own ultra-stylised world. It's one of those games that has to be experienced to really 'get it'. If you haven't done so yet, you should.

Infinity Blade II

Price: £4.99
Developed By: Chair Entertainment
In-app Purchases: Yes

Chair's sequel revisits the approach of its predecessor, but with greater combat variety and more detailed graphics. At times, when the screen fills with flesh and armour and you're swiping away wildly, it can feel a little like slicing chunks of meat wrapped in tinfoil. However, its structure constantly encourages you to have just one more battle; when you look up and realise it's 2am, you'll know you're hooked all over again, and the graphics really have to be seen to be believed.

Where's My Water

Price: £0.69
Developed By: Disney
In-app Purchases: No

Disney have hit gold with this top drawer puzzler, in which you need to channel water past various obstacles and into the shower head of clean freak alligator, Swampy. The premise is silly, the gameplay is addictive and highly challenging. As with all the best puzzlers, it starts off simple and eases you into the routine of things before turning up the heat and that's when things really start to get interesting. Behind the cartoony presentation is a very solid puzzle mechanic indeed.

Fruit Ninja

Price: £0.99
Developed By: Halfbrick Studios
In-app Purchases: No

In many ways Fruit Ninja is the archetypal touch screen game. It's a very simple reaction test, but soon gets challenging. Slice and dice fruit by swiping while avoiding the bombs. It's as simple, and yet, as difficult as that. Going for the big high scores is what it's all about and this is what will keep you coming back to it time and again. It's unashamedly shallow but perfect for the format and looks great visually. It also takes a lot more skill than you might first think.

Broken Sword: DC

Price: £2.99
Developed By: Revolution Software
In-app Purchases: No

After years gathering dust, the rise of touchscreen gaming has resurrected the classic point and click adventure genre. The Broken Sword series rests fondly in our hearts and now you can revisit it all over again. These games were somewhat under-appreciated in their day, so it's great to have the chance to experience this one once more. It's also a format that's perfectly suited to the iPad and it looks and plays brilliantly. More of this sort of thing, please!

Jurassic Park Builder

Price: Free
Developed By: Ludia Inc
In-app Purchases: Yes

Think you can create your own dinosaur park and not have the dinosaurs escape and eat everyone? Now's your chance to prove it with Jurassic Park builder. This is a great use of the licence, which fits perfectly with the resource management style of gameplay. Collect resources and save up for cooler, bigger and more fearsome dinosaurs and share your park with others via Game Centre. Top Jurassic larks, although it is rather slow paced.

Modern Combat 3

Price: £2.99
Developed By: Gameloft
In-app Purchases: Yes

A good deal of Gameloft's success is based on taking the biggest console titles and translating them to mobile formats. Arguably the biggest console franchise of them all is Call of Duty: Modern Warfare, and Modern Combat 3 is a blood-pumping, chest-thumping military FPS in exactly the same mould. The controls need a little practice in order to run and gun effectively, but this is an issue that will always be inherent in the touch screen format.

Once you get to grips with it, you'll be astonished by the quality of the graphics. The 3D world is beautifully rendered and runs smoothly even as explosions detonate around you.

A good size single player campaign (8-10 hours worth) is on offer along with multiplayer death match, which also works surprisingly well. Now you don't have to be tethered to your TV in order to shoot your friends!

If you're a Call of Duty junkie who can't bare to be away from the game for too long then Modern Combat 3 offers the perfect way to get your fix on the move. It's a remarkable technical achievement, although it does suffer from some control issues. Get past these though and you're in for a treat.

Dead Trigger

Price: Free
Developed By: MADFINGER Games
In-app Purchases: No

Hosing zombie hordes with lead just never seems to get old, no matter how many times one does it. Never has zombie slaying looked as good on a mobile device as it does in Dead Trigger. The graphics here are truly stunning and come to life on the screen in all their grisly, bloody glory. The game itself is a fairly standard first person shooter in which you need to gun down the undead as they come for you. Tight controls and the aforementioned amazing graphics are what make Dead Trigger stand out in a crowded genre.

Football Manager Handheld

Price: £6.99
Developed By: SEGA of America
In-app Purchases: No

If you're a football fan and you've never experienced Football Manager, then you've missed out on one of the most compelling and consuming gaming experiences available. Although not quite as feature-packed as the PC and Mac versions, Football Manager Handheld retains all the qualities that have turned this game into a second life for so many people. Whether you want to take a top team and build a dynasty or drag a lower league club to glory; wheel and deal in the transfer market or promote youth players, you can do it your way.

Campus Life

Price: Free
Developed By: Pocket Gems Inc
In-app Purchases: Yes

Here's one for the girly gamers out there. The aim is to create the most popular sorority on campus and you do this by recruiting the hottest girls and buying the hottest clothes, throwing parties, fitting out your home with all the latest gadgets and coolest furniture, helping the local puppy rescue centre (yes, really) and assorted other tasks. Every action costs in-game currency which can be earned (slowly) or purchased with real money to speed the game up. Younger girls who like designing and dressing up avatars will love it.

Your iPad Air And Gaming

Hero Academy

Price: Free
Developed By: Robot Entertainment
In-app Purchases: Yes

DEFEAT YOUR ENEMIES!

Robot Entertainment's staff has plenty of tactical nous, with the likes of *Age of Empires* and *Halo Wars* on their CVs. It shows in this multiplayer-only turn-based strategy game, albeit one that reverses an iOS standard – instead of collecting gems, your objective is to smash them.

The alternative to destroying your rival's crystals is to annihilate them, though the violence is gentle and cartoonish as fantasy archetypes battle it out on a series of rudimentary 9x5 grids. The characters might be clichéd, but they're well-drawn and designed in a way that makes their type (healer, mage, warrior) instantly obvious.

Each player has five moves per turn. In addition to moving and attacking, you can apply offensive and defensive buffs, cast spells and revive fallen troops.

Even with a variety of very different teams (the Council can be used on the free download, but you'll have to pay for the Dark Elves, the Dwarves and the Tribe), it's a well-balanced effort, and the interface is so crisp it's simply a joy to play.

Symphonica

Price: Free
Developed By: Square Enix
In-app Purchases: Yes

Help wannabe conductor Takt fulfil his dreams in this anime-style music game. You'll need to make sure your orchestra is under control and sounding great in order to progress. There are about 50 different pieces of classical music built into the game, and you'll need to master them all to succeed. Unlike *Rock Band*, you can't pick and choose here; the music is part of the story and you need to play through each piece in turn. Conducting is more difficult than it looks, and you'll gain a new appreciation for that through playing *Symphonica*. Plus it looks gorgeous.

Words With Friends HD

Price: £1.99/ $2.99
Developed By: Zynga Mobile
In-app Purchases: Yes (tokens)

It's Scrabble by another name. Produced in response to a lack of an online multiplayer mode in the officially licensed Electronic Arts app, *Words With Friends* enables users to connect to friends and random opponents anywhere in the world. It plays pretty much identically to the word game you all know and love, but it benefits enormously from a clear, readable, user-friendly interface and sensible options, even down to the ability to simply shake to rearrange your tiles. Little wonder it's one of the most popular word games on iOS.

Tiny Tower

Price: Free
Developed By: NimbleBit
In-app Purchases: Yes (Tower 'Bux')

Running laundromats, arcades, cake shops and sushi bars, the 'bitizens' of *Tiny Tower* are a busy bunch and it's up to you to help make their businesses a success by bowing to their every whim. You'll need to match their abilities to an appropriate role, ensure products are regularly stocked and ferry non-workers about. You're essentially doing fairly menial tasks that all amount to pressing buttons over and over again, but that won't stop you from picking up your iPad every ten minutes to see how your pixelated people are getting along. It's worryingly addictive.

Metal Slug 1

Price: £2.49
Developed By: SNK PLAYMORE
In-app Purchases: No

Metal Slug 1, 2, 3 and X are all available to buy in the App Store but there's something about the original that makes it extra special. Metal Slug is a wildly over the top shooter which owes much to the side-scrolling arcade games of yesteryear. It combines chunky cartoon graphics and a very cool art-style with some of the most maddeningly difficult, frustrating and violent action you can imagine. The screen can become engulfed in bullets and explosions as the enemy throw their considerable might at you, and just surviving the first mission is an achievement in itself. This conversion is first class and looks perfect. The only real issue is with the control. The game was obviously designed for a joystick and with the difficulty level pitched fairly close to insane, the reduced precision of touch-screen control can be highly frustrating at times. Despite this problem, Metal Slug is still great fun and the iOS version retains all the charm of the original. If you're the sort of person who enjoys blowing things up with gay abandon, you'll love it. Just remember to take deep breaths when you feel the frustration levels rising.

Incoboto

Price: £2.49 / $3.99
Developed By: Fluttermind
In-app Purchases: No

This charmingly elegant puzzle-platformer – brainchild of Dene Carter, co-creator of the Fable series – is full of clever and darkly humorous moments. You play a diminutive astronaut, exploring an empty universe with the last remaining sun, returning light to the worlds you visit as you go. Its physics-powered and gravity-controlled conundrums are often real head-scratchers, the virtual touch controls are smartly calibrated to not annoy and the story carries more emotional weight than you might think. A real gem in every sense of the word.

SongPop

Price: £1.49 / $1.99
Developed By: FreshPlanet
In-app Purchases: Yes (credits)

Can you identify a random tune or artist more quickly than your friends? Find out with *SongPop*, a music guessing game in which being able to correctly identify a song one tenth of a second more quickly than your friend can be the difference between winning and losing. The more games you win, the more coins you earn, and the more coins you have, the more playlists you can unlock. *SongPop* caters for all musical tastes, so if you're an expert on metal while your friends are mostly into jazz, you can choose the kind of music you like.

Radballs

Price: £1.99 / $2.99
Developed By: Glow Play
In-app Purchases: No

It may be yet another puzzle, but *Radballs* is the game the cool kids play. Well, probably. It's an impossibly hip concoction with an aesthetic pieced together from every 80s electronica album cover ever made and pulsing techno tunes from former Nintendo composer Neil Voss. Fortunately, there's substance behind the style, with a blob-matching puzzler that echoes Tetsuya Mizuguchi's Lumines and the reactive soundtrack makes you feel like a DJ as you expertly scratch matched orbs as a bar descends with the beat to remove them.

iPad Air

Magnetic Billiards: Blueprint

Price: Free
Developed By: Zee-3
In-app Purchases: Yes

From game design veterans The Pickford Bros comes this wonderfully eccentric title that blends puzzle games with ball sports to great effect. Although the inclusion of billiards in the title might suggest otherwise, your job isn't to pot the balls, but to fire them into groups of four or more to remove them from play. To maximize your score you'll need to pull off trick shots that bounce off walls around the table, building your combo by narrowly missing other balls and then landing clusters of specific shapes.

It may seem confusing at first (although the built-in tutorial is well laid-out), but after a while the mechanics will become second nature and you'll soon be racking up the S-ranks. Then you'll unlock the Serious tables, which is where the real challenge begins.

As if that weren't enough, there are also several further variant modes that require almost the exact opposite approach, as you endeavour to clear the table quickly before it becomes too crowded due to new balls appearing after every turn you take.

What sets Magnetic Billiards apart from the many puzzle games in the App Store, however, is its rare level of polish and warm sense of humour, with cartoon images of the Pickfords and the boys themselves shouting "Marvellous!" after particularly skilful shots – although they could just as easily be describing the game itself.

Coaster Crazy

Price: Free
Developed By: Frontier Developments
In-app Purchases: Yes

Coaster Crazy casts you as a theme park developer. The crazies are ride fanatics, and in order to earn money and experience points, you'll need to build increasingly elaborate rollercoasters that meet all of their requirements. The more successful you are, the more theme parks you get to open, as the game lets you move around the world, building ever faster, and more thrilling rides. The graphics are cute and cartoony, and since the crazies are invincible, it won't matter if your rollercoaster isn't quite complete when you send them off for a test drive. Oh, and then there are the zombies…

Bumpy Road

Price: £1.99
Developed By: Simogo
In-app Purchases: No

Scandinavian developer Simogo takes us on a gentle Sunday drive with an elderly couple who pootle around in their dinky car, collecting various trinkets and photographs as they reminisce about their past. It might sound awfully twee but it's actually rather touching, both figuratively and literally. You guide the car using your finger to raise and lower the road underneath your car, which, as befitting a surface more akin to the keys of a xylophone than a strip of tarmac, plays musical notes as you touch it. Beautiful, whimsical and totally moving. Just try it, then you'll see.

Agent Dash

Price: Free
Developed By: Full Fat
In-app Purchases: Yes

Developer Full Fat is best known for its Flick sports games, but it also ventures into other genres, like this lightning-paced running game. Agent Dash might be the world's fastest secret agent. His mission is to destroy supervillains' bases, dodging obstacles and grabbing jetpacks and other handy tools along the way. Since supervillains tend to defend their top-secret hideaways, you'll have to navigate all sorts of perils, from boiling lava to lethal laser beams. You probably won't want to play it for hours on end, but it's fun enough to dip in and out of, and the slick graphics set it apart from similar games.

Burnout CRASH!

Price: £2.99
Developed By: Criterion Games
In-app Purchases: No

Criterion's fender-bending downloadable console hit finally arrives in the App Store with a fresh lick of paint and, in its natural habitat, it's even more addictive than ever.

There really wasn't an awful lot wrong with *Burnout CRASH!*'s debut on Xbox Live Arcade; it merely felt like a game on the wrong format. Now, though, it's finally arrived on the format that it originally seemed to be made for, and it's a perfect fit.

The objective remains the same: steer your vehicle into a junction and attempt to annihilate as many automobiles as you can, though Criterion has made a few changes to the formula. The structure has been tweaked for starters. The divisive Road Block mode, which players had to complete before others were unlocked is now third on the list rather than first, though the modes can be played in any order.

It seems the difficulty has been tweaked too, although perhaps that's partly down to the touch controls, which make flinging your car about easier and more intuitive than ever. Hitting a single car gradually increases your Crashbreaker meter and when filled you can trigger an explosion, swiping to manoeuvre your vehicle to cause as much damage as possible. Even when the meter is empty, you can bunny-hop closer to your chosen target.

The upshot is that Road Block instantly becomes much more enjoyable. While you're still tasked with preventing five cars from passing through the junction unscathed, it's far simpler to obstruct their exit and thus build your way up to the special features that really rack up the points. Hit a pizza van and you'll be asked to spin a wheel for a random bonus, while letting an ambulance pass to safety removes a single cross from your tally of escapee vehicles. Nabbing a magnet attracts all vehicles to your location, allowing you to create chain reactions and earn bonuses, while pushing cars into sinkholes nets you further cash.

Last long enough and you'll earn that area's super feature: these range from plane crashes and tornadoes to tsunamis and even flying saucers, and they will usually net you the star for passing the final points tally for that stage. There are five stars to earn for each junction, and these unlock new levels and additional vehicles to play with.

Above: Hey kids, remember that exploding is good for you!

Above: Can you create the biggest pile-up ever? Of course you can!

Pile Up mode isn't quite as much fun, asking you to crash a certain number of cars before burning them up for big bucks. Instead, Rush Hour is the real winner, giving you a full 90 seconds to wreak all kinds of havoc without fear of penalty.

It's this mode you'll likely return to for high-score attempts, and EA's Autolog allows you to view and compete against your friends' totals as you battle for leaderboard supremacy. It does require you to sign up to the publisher's Origin service, but it's worth it, because it's here that the real longevity lies once you've conquered all the junctions in your favourite modes.

Thankfully, *Burnout CRASH!* remains as gaudy, brash and silly as it was on its XBLA debut. This is a game where Spandau Ballet's 'Gold' plays when you hit a glittering car, where Gloria Estefan's 'Dr. Beat' heralds an ambulance's arrival and where Shirley Bassey sings when a bank van goes boom. It's bright, fun and wonderfully cathartic, and it's accessible to players of all skill levels.

Anyone with an appetite for iOS destruction should race onto the App Store and download it now.

Your iPad Air And
Productivity

The iPad's potential as a source of entertainment is covered at length elsewhere in this guide, but don't underestimate its power as a serious tool for work and business. Apple's iWork is a suite of three apps that cover presentations, word-processing and spreadsheets, and we've got in-depth tutorials on all three. The first is Keynote, which enables you to create slide show presentations on any subject complete with moving elements and fancy transitions. Pages is a beautiful word processor that does a lot more than check your spelling. With it, you can create beautiful documents with images and other elements. It's ideal for everything from projects to job applications. Last but not least is Numbers – a powerful spreadsheet app. All three iWork apps come with a wide range of templates which can be customised to create beautiful and effective documents with ease. Our tutorials will guide you through each one. We've also selected a few of the top productivity apps for you as well.

"All three iWork apps come with a wide range of templates which can be customised to create beautiful and effective documents with ease"

92 iWork
- Pages – more than just word processing
- Numbers – keeping your figures in order
- Keynote – presentations done the iPad way

93 How To Use Keynote
- Create A New Presentation
- Adding Slides
- Adding And Editing Text

93 How To Use Keynote (continued)
- Adding And Removing Elements
- Moving Elements
- Adding Content To A Slide
- Transitions
- Magic Move And Play Back
- Share Your Presentation

96 How To Use Pages
- Create A New Document And Start Writing
- Choosing Fonts And Adding Images
- Apply A New Style
- Share, Print, Help And Security

98 How To Use Numbers
- Numbers With iCloud
- Create A Blank Spreadsheet
- Adding Information
- Insert A Chart And Applying Styles
- Exporting Data

100 Productivity Apps
- iTemplates
- Polaris Office
- Templates For Numbers
- TeamViewer
- Notability
- SimpleMind+
- abc Notes
- Brushes – iPad Edition
- Captain Dash
- The Wedding Planner

Price: £6.99 per app (Pages, Numbers, Keynote)
Developed By: Apple
In-app Purchases: No

Above: Pages can be used to create professional documents

Ordinarily the three apps that make up iWork – Keynote, Numbers and Pages – cost £6.99 each, but if you've bought a new iOS device you can get them all for free!

Everyone has heard of Microsoft Office. Word, Excel and PowerPoint are pretty much the standard word processor, spreadsheet creator and presentation editor for most people in business. Apple has it's own set of apps though, and they're perfectly tailored to make use of the iPad's advanced technology and functionality. Collectively these apps are known as iWork. iWork consists of Pages (a powerful and flexible word processor), Numbers (an intuitive spreadsheet app) and Keynote (which enables you to create amazing-looking presentations in minutes).

Every device needs a decent word processor. From composing letters and emails to projects, essays and creative writing, there's so much you might want to do with it. That's where Pages comes in, but it's much more than just a spelling and grammar checker. Flexible in-built design options and a wide array of pre-made templates mean even a complete novice can create something that looks really professional. It could be a press pack for a small business or a menu for a dinner party, you can make it easily in Pages and it's guaranteed to look the part.

So, if pages has the wordy side of things locked down, what about the numbers? Well, that's where Numbers comes in, obviously! Spreadsheets can appear rather daunting if you've never used one before, but once you get the concept they can be incredibly handy. They enable you to organise just about anything from projects to finances. The beauty of Numbers is that it does most of the hard work for you. Your spreadsheets can be as simple or as complex as you like. Just work at a level that you're comfortable with and you'll be fine. Once you get the hang of it you can present your data using a range of cool graphics, charts and even 3D graphics that come built into numbers. These can be used to great visual effect while also enabling you to see data more clearly.

Last but not least in the iWork triumvirate is Keynote. If you've ever seen a PowerPoint presentation, you'll understand straight away what it's all about. You can put

Above: Keynote can show off those new holiday snaps!

together presentations based on a series of slides that enable you to present an idea or concept. You do this with various different elements including graphics and images as well words. An extensive selection of templates enable you to put something together in very little time at all by just editing the place-holder text and adding your own pictures in place of the sample images. If you want to get more creative, you can. An impressive variety of animated transition effects can be applied for when flicking between slides and these can make a presentation look very flash and professional indeed.

It's a nice gesture by Apple to make these excellent apps available for free to people who've bought a new iOS device. They all serve different purposes, but the one thing that can be said of all the iWork apps is that they're a joy to use. The interfaces of all three are simple and intuitive to use. Once you get the hang of the basics you'll soon be using them like a pro. If you don't want to get into the nuts and bolts, you don't have to. Apple has thoughtfully included all the templates you need to produce pretty much anything you want. If you do want to have more control though, then the scope is incredibly broad for all three apps. If you haven't got the message yet, go and download Numbers, Pages and Keynote now!

How To Use... Keynote

Create amazing presentations using words, pictures and awesome transitions in just a few minutes.
Keynote makes it all so very easy.

Step 1: Create A New Presentation

When you start Keynote, you'll see the Presentation library screen that stores all your created documents for easy access. Hit the plus button in the top-left corner and choose Create Presentation to start a new file, then pick a theme from the pre-loaded selection. White and Black are blank slates for you to start from.

Step 2: Adding Slides

Keynote's edit screen is split into the editing window, which displays each slide as it'll appear in your final presentation, and the Navigator, which shows a library of the slides you've made. Tap the plus button in the bottom-left corner to create a new slide. You'll see a selection of slide templates to choose from, although these are all totally open to editing.

How To Use… Keynote (continued)

Step 3: Adding And Editing Text

As you can probably guess, adding text to a slide is as simple as double-tapping the text box and then typing away on the virtual keyboard. Keynote also works with Dictation. To select parts of the text for editing purposes, double-tap to select a specific word or triple-tap to highlight an entire paragraph of text.

Step 4: Adding And Removing Elements

While the slide templates offer a handy guide, you can alter them at will by adding more elements or deleting existing ones. To add more text or picture boxes, tap one and select Copy from the option bar, then tap on a blank space and tap Paste to replicate that element. To delete something, tap it and choose the Delete option.

Step 5: Moving Elements

To move an element, just tap and hold on it, before dragging it into the right position. Resizing any element is done by selecting it and then dragging the blue dots around. If you tap another element while resizing, Keynote will resize it to match the one you touched. You can also rotate elements by touching with two fingers and twisting.

Step 6: Adding Content To A Slide

There are two ways of adding images to your slides: either import them as new elements or drop them into pre-existing picture boxes. To do the latter, just tap the box and choose Replace from the options, then select the right image from your Camera Roll. You can also add content from the toolbar such as Media, Tables, Charts and Shapes.

iTIP – SAVING TO ICLOUD
As with other iWork apps, Keynote can link to iCloud to back up and share your documents. You can turn this on/off in the Apps > Keynote section of Settings.

Step 7: Transitions

Tap the Tools (spanner) icon and choose Transitions and Builds to add effects to your slides. Transitions are the changeover effects from one slide to another, such as dissolving and fading. Builds relate to elements and let you animate text boxes on the page or swap from one picture to another using the same image box on a single slide.

Step 8: Magic Move

Magic Move is an advanced transition technique; choose it and the slide you're viewing will be duplicated. Then, using this duplicate, move the elements on the slide around or even add new ones. When you play the presentation, the transition between the two slides will see all the elements move around as you dictated.

Step 9: Play Back

To run your presentation as a slideshow, just press the play button in the top-right corner. By default, you'll need to tap the screen to advance slides, but you can set it to run automatically in the Tools > Advanced > Presentation Type menu. You can also set the iPad to work with an Apple Remote under the Advanced > Remote menu.

Step 10: Share Your Presentation

You can share your finished presentation in several ways. Obviously you can just play it on your iPad or hook it up to a TV or bigger display. You can also email your presentation, send it to a printer, copy it into your iTunes, or share it in other ways by touching the Share and Print option in the Tools menu.

iPad Air

How To Use... Pages

Pages enables you to create beautiful, professional-looking documents and projects with different fonts, text-styles, images and no design skills required!

Step 1: Create A New Document

When you first start Pages, you'll be sent to the Documents screen, which will be empty initially but as you start creating new files, they'll appear here. Tap the plus button in the top left and choose Create Document to make a new file, then select from one of the many starter templates or just choose Blank if you want to start afresh without any further assistance.

Step 2: Start Writing

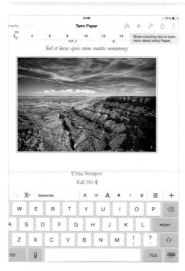

Writing with Pages is a piece of cake. Just touch the page to place the cursor and then type with the virtual keyboard that appears. If you're using a template, you'll see placeholder text. Just touch it and start typing. By default, the Word Count and Check Spelling settings will be, but you can turn these off by tapping the spanner icon and going into Settings.

iTIP – FOLDERS IN PAGES

Tap and hold on a file on the Documents screen, then drag files together to create folders. This way you can help keep your Pages documents organised.

Step 3: Choosing Fonts

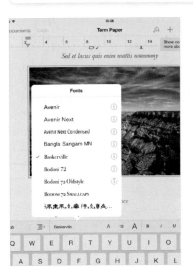

To select any text, double-tap it or triple-tap if you want to select an entire paragraph. There's a ruler at the top of the screen and a bar above the keypad contains short-cuts for text styling. You can use these to change the font, increase the size of the text, apply bold, italic or underline styles and alter the alignment, as well as adding hard tabs if you need them.

Step 4: Adding Images

If you want to add a picture to your document, tap where you'd like it to appear to move the cursor there, then touch the plus button on the top bar. From here, you can choose any photo that's in your Camera Roll or Photo Stream, as well as a variety of tables, charts and shapes. You can then move and resize the image by dragging the blue dots.

Step 5: Apply A New Style

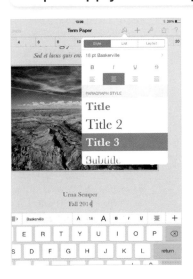

Tap an element on the page, then tap the paintbrush icon on the top bar to apply style changes. The options you get will be context-sensitive depending on what you've selected, such as borders for photos or colours for charts, as well as flipping, scaling and more. Style application also applies to text, as there are a variety of stock text styles like headings or titles.

Step 6: Share, Print, Help And Security

There are three icons at the top right of the screen to try out. The question mark gives on-screen help, the arrow icon enables you to share the existing document through available channels, while the spanner opens up the settings. Have a browse through these yourself. They enable you to set Pages up to your own specifications and also to add a security password.

iPad Air

How To Use... Numbers

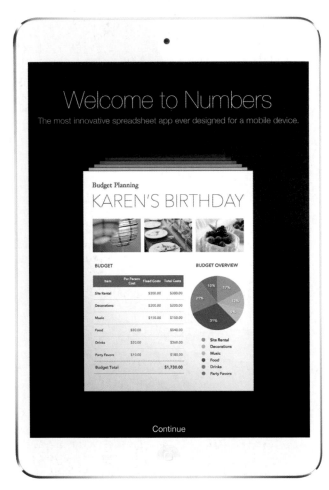

Effective use of spreadsheets enables you to organise everything from house chores to finances. Apple's Numbers provides you with an elegant spreadsheet solution for iPad.

Step 1: Numbers With iCloud

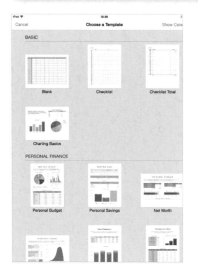

When you first start up Numbers, you'll get the option to activate iCloud and share all the documents you create within it with all your other iOS devices. Obviously, it makes sense to say yes so that everything you do is backed up in case something goes wrong, but you can always go into Settings and find Numbers in the Apps section later if you want to turn it off.

Step 2: Create A Blank Spreadsheet

Select the Create A New Spreadsheet option (or tap Spreadsheets in the top-left corner and then hit the plus button) and you'll get to choose from all manner of pre-loaded templates. Start with a blank one for now. If you want to add another sheet to your document, just tap the plus symbol tab at the top left. To re-order sheets, hold a tab and drag it left or right.

iTIP – GET COMFORTABLE
Numbers can be as simple or as complex as you like. The Getting Started file on the main spreadsheet page has interactive tutorials that are really useful.

Step 3: Adding Information

To add content to your table, double-tap any cell to make the virtual keyboard appear. There are four different keyboards, accessed by the circular buttons. '42' offers digits, money, percentages and more, Clock lets you enter dates and times, 'T' is for pure text entry and '=' is for formulas that let you add up columns/rows, calculate percentages and so on.

Step 4: Insert A Chart

Once you have a table full of data, you can automatically convert it into a chart by tapping the plus button in the top-right corner and choosing Charts. Drag the one you want to where you want it on the page, then tap the big blue button to add data. Tap and drag to select the cells you want featured in your table, then touch the Done button at the top to create the chart.

Step 5: Applying Styles

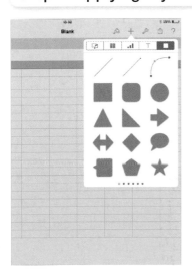

You can also change the style of virtually every element of your spreadsheet by selecting the thing you want to change, then tapping the paintbrush icon in the top-right to bring up a context-sensitive menu. Style changes range from simple things like colour or layout to more in-depth design changes – explore the menus and you'll see just how much there is to alter!

Step 6: Exporting Data

Your spreadsheet will automatically be saved in Numbers, so when you open the app again you can access your previous work from the Spreadsheets menu. If you want to be able to use this data in other apps or send it to someone else, just tap the Tools menu and you'll see you can send or print your data or save it in a format that can be opened by other programs.

iPad Air

Productivity Apps

It's a results-based world that we live in, and if there's any way you can increase your efficiency and productivity, that's got to be a good thing, right? Well your iPad can help.

iTemplates

Price: £1.99
Developed By: Abdullah
In-app Purchases: No

Even though Pages gives you the flexibility to create pretty much any kind of document you like with the templates provided, it still requires more effort than some people are willing to give. iTemplates has a huge number of pre-built templates for Pages split into different categories – CVs, letters, memos and more. You need Pages to use it, though.

Polaris Office

Price: £16.99
Developed By: Infraware Co. Ltd
In-app Purchases: No

Apple's range of iWork apps can provide the perfect word processing, spreadsheet and presentation tools for the iPad, but that doesn't mean you're stuck for choice. True, Microsoft doesn't have an Office presence on the App Store, but Polaris Office is pretty much the same thing and even supports documents created in Microsoft formats.

Templates For Numbers

Price: £1.99
Developed By: Graphic Node
In-app Purchases: No

Just as iTemplates (covered on the left) adds a wide range of new templates to Apple's Pages app, so Templates For Numbers adds templates for Numbers. There are 70 new templates available in both A4 and US Letter format that can be edited as you like, and importing them is as simple as choosing the one you want and pressing a button.

TeamViewer

Price: Free
Developed By: TeamViewer
In-app Purchases: No

This app allows secure remote access to any computers or devices connected to it, so if you want to be able to access files on your computer while you're out and about, you can via your iPad. You can even reboot your computer remotely. The free version is only for personal use, and if you're planning to use this in a commercial environment you need to shell out for the Pro version.

Notability

Price: £1.99
Developed By: Ginger Labs
In-app Purchases: No

Take notes in whatever way suits you best with Notability. The app integrates handwriting, typing and recording, so you can use whichever method you prefer to keep a record of your thoughts and ideas. You can even use it to annotate PDFs, which are otherwise tricky to edit. Notability can also sync with several cloud services, including Dropbox, to make sure there's always a backup of your work saved somewhere.

SimpleMind+

Price: Free
Developed By: xpt Software & Consulting
In-app Purchases: Yes (full version upgrade)

Have you ever tried mind mapping? It's the process of writing down ideas and then pulling ideas out from those into a giant spider-web of creativity, which comes in useful when you have a big group of people all thinking about the same thing. SimpleMind+ takes that concept and makes it digital, meaning you can create and then share mind maps at the touch of a button.

abc Notes

Price: £2.19
Developed By: Alsedi Group
In-app Purchases: No

Taking sticky notes into the future is abc Notes, designed to become your stylish and easy-to-use assistant in taking notes and managing to-do lists.

It really takes advantage of the iPad, utilising the potential of the touch screen as well as the retina display. Reassuringly, the app preserves the realistic look and feel of paper sticky notes. All your notes and desktops are seamlessly synchronised between your devices so your data is always accessible. No more tedious note lists, as abc Notes brings you the ability to make actual notes on your iPad. Now there's no excuse for forgetting those birthdays or anniversaries.

abc Notes is stylish, highly customisable, functional and easy to use which makes taking notes and managing to-do lists a piece of cake. It uses the iPad's touch screen to good effect and the notes themselves look like real stickies. This is a nice touch and makes it very appealing. And there's the added advantage that they don't get scattered everywhere when someone knocks into your desk!

Brushes – iPad Edition

Price: £5.49
Developed By: Taptrix Inc
In-app Purchases: No

As far as creative art packages go, they really don't come any more powerful than Brushes. It's an entire paint set in digital form, allowing you to use 19 different brushes and five unique blend modes across up to six different layers (meaning you can edit one part of a painting without having to mess with other bits you're happy with) to create art that's truly awe-inspiring – provided you have the necessary talent to do it, that is. It's not cheap, but if you have the urge to unleash your inner artist then you should give it some serious consideration, it's that good.

Captain Dash

Price: Free
Developed By: Captain Dash
In-app Purchases: Yes

Captain Dash performs the superhuman feat of handling complex numbers with ease. The app enables you to use your data from Google Analytics, Twitter, Facebook and Foursquare on a single platform and produce on-demand, interactive dashboards and alerts to optimise marketing decision making.
Manage your data sources and get insights for your e-business or your retail activity. This removes the secrets about SEO and point of sales analytics. With this app you can have a complete overview of your world. Try the Lite version out for free.

The Wedding Planner

Price: £6.99
Developed By: Createful Ltd
In-app Purchases: No

Organising a wedding can be an incredibly stressful business. Whether you are planning your own wedding or your daily work is to plan weddings for customers, The Wedding Planner is the organiser app that will help you create that special day. It works by allowing you to manage and keep track of all the vital information about the important day and access it easily. Keeping on top of a multitude of wedding plans couldn't be simpler. Using the app on the iPad is the best way to ensure even the smallest details aren't forgotten. But still double-check that the Best Man has the ring.

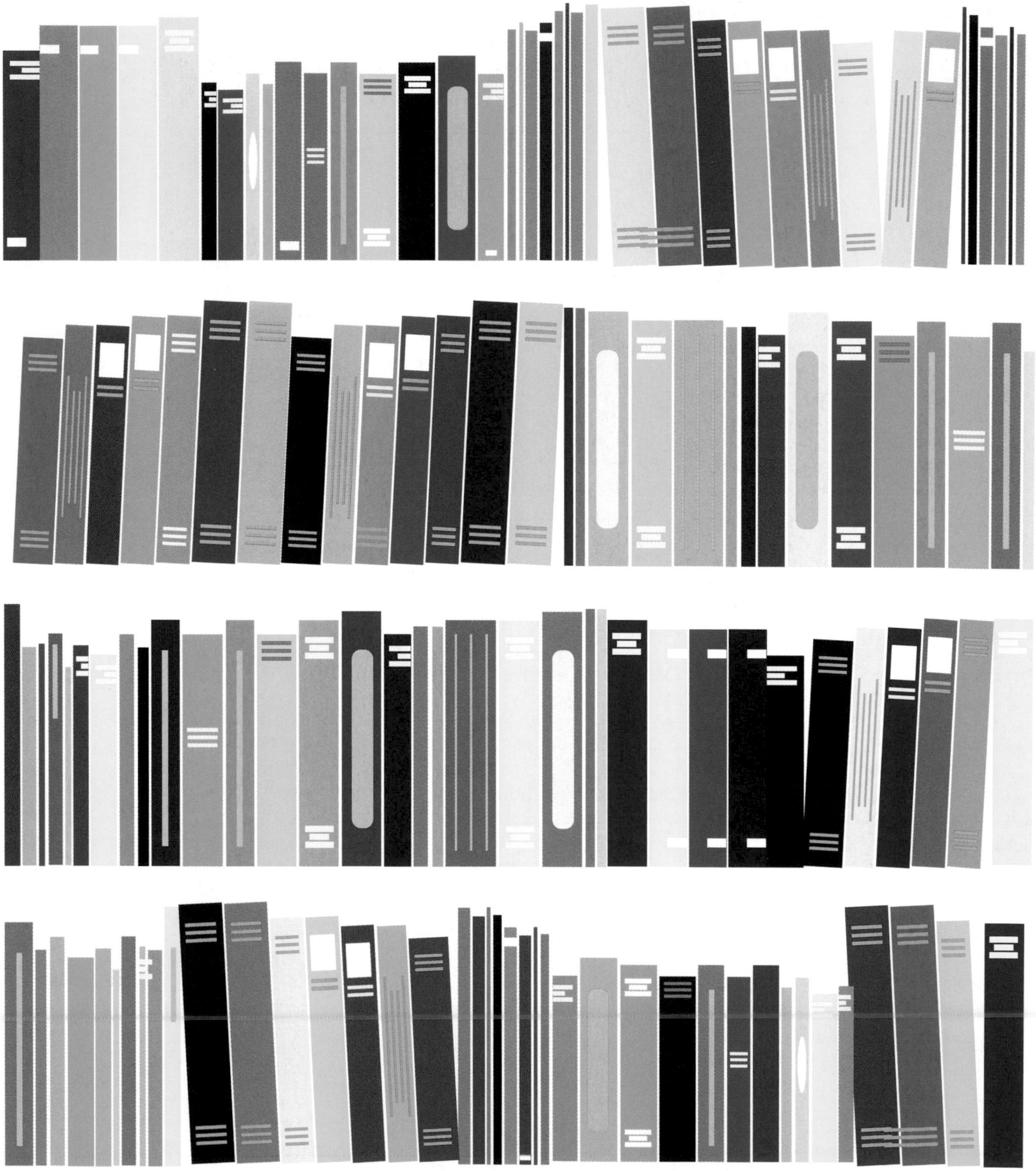

Your iPad Air And
Books and Education

Books are heavy and cumbersome to carry around with you, but thanks to the iPad you no longer have to. The iBooks store contains thousands of books from classics to the latest best-sellers and they're all available to buy and download instantly to your iPad. Our tutorial explains exactly how to use iBooks and how to read the books that you download.

Newsstand is the place to buy digital editions of all your favourite magazines, newspapers and any other periodical publications you're interested in. Our tutorial explains how to download each publication's app, how to subscribe to publications and how to manage your subscriptions.

The iPad's potential as a learning tool shouldn't be underestimated. iTunes U makes a huge amount of educational material available to everyone and the App Store is also home to a wide variety of literary and educational apps, just a few of which are rounded up at the end of this section.

"The iBooks store contains thousands of books from classics to the latest best-sellers and they're all available to buy and download instantly to your iPad"

104 How To Use iBooks

- Find New Books
- Add PDF Documents To iBooks
- Browse Your Library
- Add Bookmarks
- Text Formatting
- The Dictionary

106 How To Use Newsstand

- Downloading Publications
- Taking Out Subscriptions
- Reading Magazines
- Automatic Downloads
- Removing Publications

108 How To Use iTunes U

- Get iTunes U
- Sync Course Information
- The Course Library
- The iTunes U Catalog
- Pick Your Learning Level
- Browsing Institutions
- Searching For Specifics
- Checking Course Details
- Subscribing To A Course
- Beginning Your Course
- The Posts Tab
- Downloading and Viewing Materials
- Adding Notes

112 Books and Education Apps

- Reading Trainer
- Dictionary.com
- Wikipedia Mobile
- Waterstones For iPad
- Marvel Comics
- Maths Age 3-5
- Five Stop Story
- Ebook Reader
- Kindle
- Audiobooks from Audible

iPad Air

How To Use... iBooks

Whatever your taste in books, from modern best sellers to the classics, you'll find plenty to satisfy it on iBooks. It contains a huge library of titles ready to download instantly.

Step 1: Find New Books

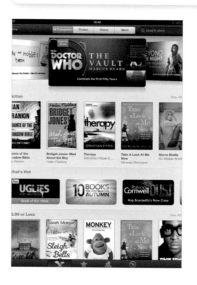

Once you download iBooks for free from the App Store, open it and tap Store in the top-left. From here you can browse or search for books, both free and paid for. Tap the grey box displaying the price, then tap it again when it turns green and enter your Apple ID. You can also tap Sample to read the first chapter if you aren't sure whether a book is for you.

Step 2: Add PDF Documents To iBooks

You can also add PDFs (a form of digital document) to iBooks. If you find a PDF online, view it through your iPad and tap it to get an Open In iBooks option. If you've been emailed a PDF, just open the attachment and tap Open In iBooks. There's an option to switch between books and PDFs under Collections at the top of the library screen.

iTip – TAKE NOTE
You can add your own notes to books by tapping and holding a word, then selecting Note. A marker then appears on the page to indicate the note.

Step 3: Browse Your Library

Once your library starts to fill up, you need an easy way to find stuff, and while the bookshelf looks nice, it's not easy to tell what's what. If you swipe down the screen you can change to list view using the icon with three horizontal lines. Then you can browse via title, author or category. You can also use the search function near the top of the screen if you have a lot of books.

Step 4: Add Bookmarks

If you have multiple Apple devices, you can use synced bookmarks to start reading on one and continue on another. Go into Settings, tap iBooks on the left and turn on 'Sync Bookmarks'. You can add bookmarks by tapping a page and then the symbol in the top-right corner. To see your bookmarks, tap the symbol on the left with the three dots and lines.

Step 5: Text Formatting

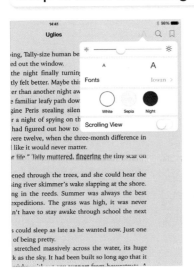

To change how the text in a book looks, tap on a page and then the symbol at the top with a small and large 'A'. On the overlay, you can alter the text size (tap the smaller or larger 'A') to make it more visible, change the font used for displaying the text and even view your books in an attractive sepia tone, which is easier for some to read than the harsher black on white.

Step 6: The Dictionary

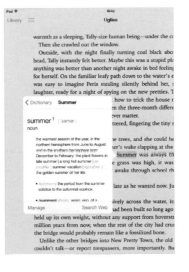

If you ever find yourself wondering what a word means, you can tap and hold your finger on any word in any book to have four different options pop up. Tapping Define from this menu will provide a definition of the highlighted word, along with examples of how it can be used in everyday language, its origin and any derivatives, just like a real dictionary.

iPad Air

How To Use... Newsstand

Newsstand

Store

Newsstand is the gateway to digital versions of thousands of publications from newspapers to specialist magazines. Download, subscribe and read them all on your iPad.

Step 1: Starting Newsstand

Newsstand

Store

The Newsstand app comes preloaded on your iPad and you'll find it right on the home screen, waiting for you. The iOS 7 version of Newsstand looks quite a lot different to previous iterations but it works in a very similar way. When you open it up for the first time you'll see an empty set of shelves just waiting to be filled up with the publications that you want to read, so let's get some.

Step 2: Downloading Publications

Note that Newsstand isn't an app; it just enables you to browse for publication apps and store them in one place. To do this, tap the Store button in the bottom corner. When you find something you want, tap the box that says Free, then tap it again when it turns green and enter your Apple ID. Just don't browse using the bottom bar, because it takes you to the main App Store!

iTip – BROWSE BY CATEGORY
Newsstand features thousands of publications in many genres. Click on Categories in the Newsstand store to discover titles you might be interested in.

Step 3: Taking Out Subscriptions

Unfortunately, each app's subscription method is different depending on the publisher concerned. Some offer pages to try out for free, but you'll always be presented with subscription options should you choose to read any regularly. Merely downloading the app doesn't subscribe you. That requires your Apple ID, so you can't do it by accident.

Step 4: Reading Magazines

You can navigate issues of a publication by swiping the screen from page to page. Details will differ of course per app, but you may be able to zoom in on text or use a dedicated read mode that shows plain copy when activated. There'll also be a contents area to allow you to navigate through the magazine. Look out for icons that activate rich media or interactive features.

Step 5: Automatic Downloads

You can set your subscribed publications up to download new issues in the background as and when they come out. This is done slightly differently from the way it was done in iOS 6. Open up Settings and tap General, then touch the Background App Refresh option. From here you can toggle automatic downloads on and off for all publications to which you subscribe.

Step 6: Removing Publications

To delete apps that you've downloaded from within Newsstand, tap and hold one of the apps until they all start to jiggle, then simply tap the X button that appears at the top left of the app. Of course, you also have to set the subscription to stop renewing within the app itself before you do this, because just deleting the app from your iPad won't end the subscription.

How To Use... iTunes U

The iPad isn't all about fun. There are plenty of serious and practical applications available too. iTunes U makes a wealth of educational material and lectures available.

Step 1: Get iTunes U

Although the name suggests that iTunes U should come pre-loaded on your iPad, it's actually available for download from the App Store. The good news is that it's free, which is always good. You can find it easily. Just do a search for iTunes U and download it. When you've got it all safely installed and ready to go, come right back here. Have you done it? Good. On to step 2.

Step 2: Sync Course Information

When you first start up iTunes U, you'll be asked to allow it to send you push notifications (which is handy for when new coursework becomes available) and to sync your notes/course information. Syncing makes all of your study materials available on all your iOS devices, so it can be very useful. You can always turn it on or off via the Settings menu later, if you change your mind.

Step 3: The Course Library

The first screen might look familiar if you've used iBooks or Newsstand; it's a storage library that shows all the courses that you've downloaded using the app. Initially, it'll be empty, unless you have previously stored work on another iOS device, in which case it'll sync the information in the account to match. To start filling it up, you'll need to pay a visit to the iTunes U catalog.

Step 4: The iTunes U Catalog

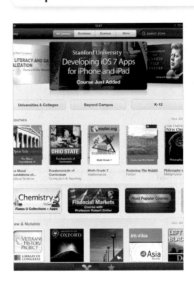

Not surprisingly, the iTunes U catalogue, which you can access by pressing the Catalog button in the top-left corner of the library screen, is much like the App and iTunes stores. The main screen shows you new courses and those that are proving to be popular, as well as a selection of promoted topics, but you can also search depending on what you're passionate about or interested in.

Step 5: Pick Your Learning Level

The catalog is split into three levels of learning: 'Universities & Colleges', 'Beyond Campus' and 'K-12'. The first speaks for itself, while the second is aimed at wider learning from places like art institutes and academies. K-12 refers to lower-level learning ranging from nursery to college students. Each offers a wide range of institutions for you to learn from.

Step 6: Browsing Institutions

To check out the different institutions available on iTunes U, just tap one of the three buttons on the front page to bring up a scrollable menu. The majority of institutions are US-based (including famous ones like Yale and Harvard), although there are others from around the world in there too. Tap a name to see all the courses available from that institution.

iPad Air

How To Use... iTunes U (continued)

Step 7: Searching For Specifics

You can search for courses in two ways: either use the Categories button on any institution to browse through subjects or tap the Search tab in the top-right and type something in. This will bring up a list of courses that match your search. Keep it as simple as possible though, because being too specific will obviously give you fewer results to look through.

Step 8: Checking Course Details

To read more about a particular course, simply tap it and you'll get a detailed information screen giving more background, a course outline showing all the modules and any reviews it has been given by other iTunes U users. You can also tap the Materials button to see what kind of things are available, for example: documentation, coursework and video tutorials.

Step 9: Subscribing To A Course

When you've found a course that you want to download, hit the grey Subscribe Free button and then Get Course when it turns green. This then adds the course list to your library shelf, but it doesn't download any of the content for that course; you do that yourself from within the course content. You can return to the library by tapping the Library button in the top-left of the store.

Step 10: Beginning Your Course

Tap the course book on your library shelf to open it and you can get learning! You'll see four tabs down the side: Info gives you details of your course (tap the Info button at the top to see more), Posts gives you a list of lessons available, Notes is where you can write your own notes (obviously!) and Materials enables you to download the various materials needed for the course.

iTip – CAN'T STAND THE HEAT?
To delete courses from your iTunes U library, tap Edit in the top-right corner of the screen, then select the ones to be removed and hit Delete in the top-left.

Step 11: The Posts Tab

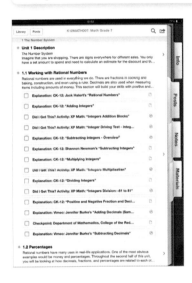

Not surprisingly, you'll spend most of your time on the Posts tab, as it's here that you can access each stage of your chosen course. Tap the arrow on the right of a lesson to see a full explanation, as well as a list of the materials necessary to aid you in your academic studies. You can tap the small checkbox next to each material to keep tabs on those you've already checked out.

Step 12: Downloading Materials

Although you can download materials in the Materials tab, it's best done from within the lesson descriptions on the Posts tab so you know which you currently need. Tap a material to expand it; you can tap the Info button to get more information or the arrow button to download it to your iPad. Make sure that you have enough storage space for all those video tutorials!

Step 13: Viewing Materials

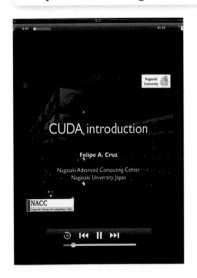

Once your materials have downloaded (which might take a while if it's a video tutorial), you can view them by tapping the relevant section. Documents and transcripts open in iBooks, PDFs open within iTunes U itself and video tutorials open with the Video app. You can also view them outside of iTunes U using these apps from the home screen.

Step 14: Adding Notes

Chances are you'll want to take notes of your own throughout the duration of your course. While you can do that with good old pen and paper, iTunes U also lets you do it digitally. Just tap the Notes tab inside any course book and then press the plus button in the top-right corner and type away on the virtual keyboard. It also supports Dictation, so you can think out loud!

Books and Education Apps

The iPad is a godsend for readers, with so many great apps to explore and enjoy. It can also be a hugely powerful educational tool for young kids, university students and anyone else who loves to learn.

Reading Trainer

Price: £2.99
Developed By: HeKu IT
In-app Purchases: No

Taking the opportunity to read more? Well, good for you. That said though, you may need to brush up on your skills if it's been a while, which is where this app comes in handy. Reading Trainer is a highly acclaimed, award-winning app that can greatly increase your reading speed and mental capacity with a variety of exercises, plus a plan that charts your progress.

Dictionary.com

Price: Free
Developed By: Dictionary.com, LLC
In-app Purchases: No

Really, this is something that everyone should have a use for, but it's especially useful for students. This dictionary app contains definitions for a million words, plus 90,000 synonyms and antonyms in the thesaurus (and let's face it, if you just had to look up 'antonym' to find out what we meant, this is definitely for you). Best of all, it doesn't require an Internet connection to work.

Wikipedia Mobile

Price: Free
Developed By: Wikimedia
In-app Purchases: No

You'd have to be living in a cave not to have heard of Wikipedia. This app gives quick access to the free encyclopaedia containing more than 20 million articles in 280 languages. Since its creation in 2001, Wikipedia has grown rapidly into one of the largest reference websites, attracting 470 million unique visitors monthly and you can add to that number!

Waterstones For iPad

Price: Free
Developed By: Waterstones
In-app Purchases: Yes

If you're a proper student at a real educational institution and have a desperate need for printed studying material, Waterstones (yes, the book store) has the app for you. Use it to browse and buy a huge range of books for delivery to your home, check stock in your local stores in case you want to go and pick it up yourself and even write reviews for your books when you're done with them.

Marvel Comics

Price: Free
Developed By: Marvel Comics
In-app Purchases: Yes

Download hundreds of Marvel Comic books featuring your favourite characters. Experience Marvel's greatest stories like never before, with your choice of guided view (an animated, panel-by-panel path through the comic) or by using regular controls to zoom and pan your way through pages of sizzling stories and amazing artwork. If you're a fan, you can't afford to be without this.

Maths Age 3-5

Price: Free
Developed By: Eurotalk
In-app Purchases: Yes

Giving your kids a leg-up on learning is always a good idea before they head to school, so this pre-school app comes in handy for getting them ahead in maths. The free version comes with the first topic (sorting and matching) and then, if your child thinks it's great, you can purchase the other nine topics either individually for 69p or as a bundle for £5. It even has an interactive 'teacher' to help.

Five Stop Story

Price: Free
Developed By: Five Stop Story
In-app Purchases: Yes

Five Stop Story is a brilliant app aimed mainly at commuters, but really anybody can enjoy it. As the title suggests, it's all about stories. Short stories, in fact. More accurately, stories that can be read in their entirety in roughly the time it takes to travel five stops on the underground, hence the title. Not everybody is into books and even if you are, it can be frustrating to read in dribs and drabs. With a vast library of stories already available and new ones being submitted all the time, Five Stop Story will always have something for you to read, whatever your taste.

You can browse by the latest stories or the most popular and you can recommend a story to other readers simply by tapping the thumbs up button at the bottom of the screen. You can also search by authors, genres and even word count if you have such specific requirements.

A small subscription fee gets you access to the service for a full year but you can try it out for free before you part with any money, and if you're a budding writer you can even submit stories yourself. It really is a great idea, a great app and a great way to help those tedious tube journeys pass more quickly.

Ebook Reader

Price: Free
Developed By: eBooks.com
In-app Purchases: Yes

Ebook Reader is an alternative to Amazon's official Kindle app. It lets you read your favourite books on the go. Choose from a massive collection of popular books that you can download quickly and easily, including hundreds of free classics. Your library is backed up online, so your books are always accessible. You can sync your eBooks.com online bookshelf with all your devices and log in with your existing eBooks.com account. Turn pages with a tap or swipe, lock landscape or portrait mode, navigate and search within the text of the book you're reading.

Kindle

Price: Free
Developed By: Amazon Mobile LLC
In-app Purchases: Yes

The Amazon Kindle, to borrow a phrase from the great Douglas Adams, is a sort of electronic book. It has revolutionised the way we read; the handy portable reader is relatively cheap and very easy to use, with millions of eBooks, magazines and newspapers available to download, including many free ones, but if you've already got an iPad and probably a smartphone, you don't want to have to carry another electronic device around with you. That's where the official Amazon Kindle app comes in. It replicates all of the functions of the Kindle device on your iPad.

Audiobooks from Audible

Price: Free
Developed By: Audible Inc
In-app Purchases: Yes

Audio books are a great way to enjoy literature while you're doing other things, such as housework, working out at the gym or driving. Audible.com by Amazon provides over 100,000 audiobook titles, from best sellers to classics and everything in-between, which you can purchase from the Audible mobile store and listen to on your iPad. Features include chapter navigation, bookmarking, sleep mode, variable narration speed and a button-free mode. If you've got an Amazon Kindle as well, you can switch between reading and listening at any time.

iPad Air

Your iPad Air And
Photography and Video

Smartphones like the iPhone are great. They come with great cameras that enable you to snap photos and shoot videos with ease. You can't fully appreciate them on the smaller screen though, and to really enjoy them you need to view them on a computer. Not so with the iPad. You can take photos, shoot video and then enjoy it all in perfect clarity on that big, beautiful retina display.

Our tutorials will guide you through both the camera's photo and video functionality. We've also got tutorials on Apple's own photo editor – iPhoto, and the amazing iMovie. iMovie will enable you to turn your bits of footage into proper movies complete with titles, soundtracks and transitions. We've also picked out a couple of cool apps that enable you to add special effects to your videos for some really spectacular results. Read on and enjoy.

"You can take photos, shoot video and then enjoy it all in perfect, clarity on that big, beautiful retina display"

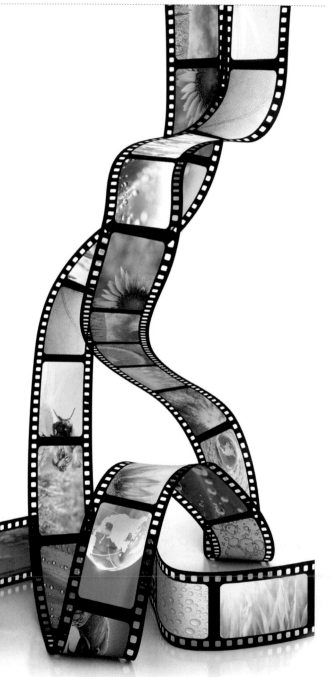

How To Use... Camera

The iPad's camera app isn't as feature-packed as the iPhone version, but it's still pretty good. Here are all the things you need to know to get snapping.

Step 1: Off To A Quick Start

The Camera app comes pre-loaded on your iPad and you just need to tap it to launch it. If you want to jump straight to the camera from the lock screen, hit the Home button then swipe the camera icon that appear in the bottom right of the screen upwards. This opens the camera app instantly – very useful if you spot a great shot but only have a few moments in which to capture it.

Step 2: Zoom

If the subject is a little bit far away or appears too small in the viewfinder, fear not, the iPad has a pretty good built-in zoom feature, although it's not obvious. Make a pinching gesture to zoom in or out. When you do so, the zoom level will appear as a marker on a bar at the bottom of the viewfinder. Drag the marker to make more accurate adjustments to the zoom level.

iTip – BAD EDITOR
If you're editing a photo and accidentally ruin it, don't worry. Just tap where it says Revert to Original at the top of the screen and all your changes will be discarded.

Step 3: Camera Controls

The camera controls are pretty simple. The icon at the top right switches between the front and back cameras, you can turn HDR on and off by tapping on HDR and you can switch between shooting modes by dragging the three options below the shutter button up and down. If you prefer, you can use either of the volume buttons instead of the on-screen shutter button.

Step 4: Changing Your Focus

The iPad has a pretty decent auto-focus feature, but it'll usually focus on the object in the middle of the screen. If you'd actually prefer to focus on something else, then it's possible to refocus the camera to whatever part of the picture you want to concentrate your shot on. Touch the object you want to focus on and the camera will do the rest for you. A box indicates the new focal point.

Step 5: Edit Photos

The most recent shot you took appears as a thumbnail at the bottom right of the screen. You can tap it to open it full screen and if you don't like it, you can discard it. You can also edit it by tapping the Edit option at the top of the screen. You'll then have the option to automatically enhance it, reduce red-eye, crop it and apply a choice of filters to make it a bit more interesting. Tap Save when done.

Step 6: Photo Storage

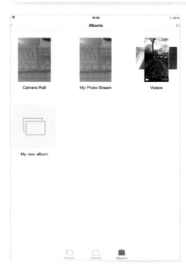

All the photos you've taken on your iPad will be stored in the Camera Roll section of the Photos App, which you'll also find sitting on your home screen. You can easily organise, share, edit or delete them from here. Due to its size, the iPad isn't an ideal camera, which might be why there are so few features in this app, but if you really need to snap a picture and it's all you have, then it'll do.

iPad Air

How To Use... Photos

The simply-named Photos is the app that enables you to organise all the downloaded images, photographs and videos that are stored on your iPad.

Step 1: Photos With iCloud

Although your iPad stores your photos safely in the Camera Roll, it's best to have a backup of everything in case something goes wrong. You can do this through iCloud; go to Settings > iCloud > Photo Stream and turn it on to keep all your photos safely stored in the cloud. You can also back up your photos to your computer using the data cable that came with your iPad, to be doubly safe!

Step 2: Creating Albums

All your photos are stored in the Photos tab of the Photos App, but to tidy things up a bit and make your photos easier to find, you might want to sort them into albums. Touch the Albums tab and you'll see just one album: Camera Roll. Touch the plus icon in the top left of the screen to make a new album, and then give it a meaningful title. You can create as many albums as you please.

iTip – POWER AND PHOTOSTREAM
If your iPad is low on juice, it will stop automatically uploading images to Photostream in order to conserve power. New images will upload when you plug it in.

Step 3: Adding Images To An Album

Once you type in a name for your album, you can select images from your iPad to add to it. Any you pick will then appear in the new album, but won't be deleted from any other albums they're in; they'll still be in Camera Roll and Photo Stream, for instance. Deleting them from these two places will delete them permanently, so be careful before choosing to do so.

Step 4: Sharing Images

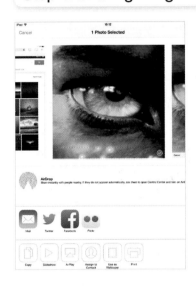

You can send and share your photos with others very easily with just a couple of taps. To send a photograph to someone else, view the image on-screen and then click on the arrow icon in the top right. You'll now have a number of options, including emailing your photo, sending it as a message, printing it out, adding it to Facebook (if you're signed in on your iPad), using it as wallpaper and more.

Step 5: Publishing Photos To Twitter

To share your images more widely than just by email or text, you can send them to Twitter straight from Photos. Selecting the 'Twitter' option will enable you to enter a short message to accompany your picture, then automatically add a Twitpic link to your image. Of course, you need to have a Twitter account set up on your iPad beforehand for this to work. See the Twitter tutorial for more details.

Step 6: More Photo Options

You can print your images using Air Print provided you have a compatible printer associated with your iPad. In addition, you can set any photograph as your wallpaper (see elsewhere in this book for full details of how to do that), or assign it to a contact, meaning that particular image will be displayed every time that person contacts you. All of these appear as sharing options.

iPhoto

Price: £2.99
Developed By: Apple
In-App Purchases: No

Above: iPhoto has a lot of sophisticated options, but most of them are really easy to work with

What GarageBand is to music and iMovie is to video, so iPhoto is to photos and images. If you want an easy way to enhance and manipulate your pictures, look no further.

Photography has become huge part of life since cameras have been built into mobile phones and tablets as standard. We've got a camera on us pretty much at all times so we tend to be snapping away a lot. If you want to make your photos look even better then you'll need a decent application with which to enhance and manipulate them. The Photoshop app from Adobe is pretty good, as you'd expect, but you really can't go wrong with Apple's own image editor. It's packed with cool functions and options that will enable you to turn your everyday snaps into works of art, and it's completely free as well! Yes, it's true. When it first came out it cost a not-inconsiderable £2.99, but the iOS 7 version has been made available free of charge to all iOS users. Apple aren't shot of a bob or two, that's for sure, but it's still a nice gesture to have made this, along with GarageBand and iMovie, free to download. Since they are free, it does seem rather odd that they don't come pre-installed with iOS 7, not that it matters of course. But enough of such musings. What is it that makes iPhoto such a damn cool app and why do you need it in your life?

It's the ease of use combined with some pretty in-depth tools that makes iPhoto on iOS 7 something special. Each of the included tools does something pretty obvious – cropping and rotating, adjusting brightness, contrast and colour, applying effects with brushes and filters – and in combination they offer a great level of control that can be used to great or subtle effect. Each function is very simple to use. A couple of touches and a few swipes are all it takes to completely change the look and feel of a photo. On the following pages we have a tutorial that takes you through how to use the various tools on offer, but in reality the best way to get comfortable with it is to play around and see for yourself which features do what.

It has plenty of other neat little touches too, such as the ability to edit the angle of your photos using the iPad's gyroscope rather than your fingers. Touching and holding

> "It's packed with cool functions and options that will enable you to turn your everyday snaps into works of art"

down two fingers brings up a magnifying lens that can then be twisted as you would a real-world lens to zoom in further and you can automatically compile selected photos into a ready-made montage of memories to show your friends. Sure, some of these features are perhaps a teeny little bit gimmicky, but it's little things like these that really set Apple's product apart from the rest of the crowd.

As you might expect, iPhoto boasts full connectivity not just with the big version of the software (that being the desktop version of iPhoto for Mac, of course), but also with a whole host of other social media sources (Facebook, Flickr, iTunes, the iPad's built-in email and more besides) that can be accessed at the touch of a virtual button. This makes it the perfect way to share your images.

It's not a professional grade tool by any means, but for such an accessible and intuitive app that can be used on the fly wherever you happen to be, iPhoto boasts an impressive array of features that offer a high level of control.

In this world of Facebook, Instagram, Flickr, Twitter and the rest, it can be hard to get your photos noticed. With the help of iPhoto you'll be able to make them appear much more striking and professional-looking regardless of your photographic or artistic ability. This should be one of the first apps you download.

How To Use... iPhoto

A good photo editor enables you to turn your average snaps into something a little bit more special, and they don't come much better than iPhoto.

Step 1: Viewing Photos In iPhoto

There's no option to take photos directly in iPhoto, but you can immediately access all the pictures in your Camera Roll and Photo Stream when you start the app. You can also import photos into iPhoto using iTunes on a computer, wirelessly beaming them from an iOS device running iPhoto or importing them from a camera (although this requires a special connection kit).

Step 2: The Thumbnail Grid

Once you select an album source for your image, you'll move to a viewing area where you can see your pictures in full. Swipe left/right on the thumbnail grid at the bottom to scroll through your images and touch one to display it. You can also see info about the photo by tapping the 'i' button in the top-right and hide the grid by tapping the small grid button, top-left.

How To Use... iPhoto (continued)

Step 3: Editing Photos

Now you've selected a picture, you can get on with editing it to your liking. The bar of icons across the bottom of the screen give you access to all the editing tools iPhoto has to offer. You can start using any of them just by tapping the one you want; once you've made adjustments, tapping the tool again closes it down and saves any changes that you may have made.

Step 4: Undo And Redo

Before you start playing around with your photos, make a note of the most important button of all: undo. It's the curved arrow on the left-hand side of the top bar (not the one in the box on the right). Tap it to undo the last action you performed or hold your finger on it to get the option to undo or redo an action. You can undo multiple steps by tapping the button more than once.

Step 5: Crop, Scale And Straighten

The first edit tool on the bottom bar is the crop tool, but it can do more than just slice into images. Using the central box as a guide, you can use one finger to find the part of your picture you want to crop around and two fingers to zoom in/out. You can also use the dial at the bottom to rotate the picture; tapping it lets you do this by tilting the iPad left or right.

Step 6: Brightness And Contrast

The next icon, which looks like a sun, enables you to make adjustments to the exposure level. You can drag the outer markers at the bottom (black for shadow, white for highlights) inwards to lighten/darken them, and the same goes for contrast and brightness. Alternatively, hold your finger on the photo to activate context-sensitive controls based on what you're touching.

iTip – SCRATCH THAT
You can return to the original version of your photo by touching the three dots at the bottom right of the screen and selecting Revert.

Step 7: Colour Adjustments

The palette icon activates the colour adjustment tools. These are split into Colour Saturation, Blue Skies, Greenery and Skin Tones and can again be slid left/right to alter the relevant part of your photo. Touching/holding on the photo once again activates context-sensitive controls and there are also white balance options under the WB icon in the bottom-right.

Step 8: Brush-based Editing

Touch the brush icon and you'll see there is a list of all the brushes you can use to touch up your photos: lighten/darken, sharpen/soften, saturate/desaturate and even one for red-eye. These effects are subtle and require direct application to the photo with a finger: Use two fingers to zoom in/out and move the photo around while applying the various different effects.

Step 9: Special Effects

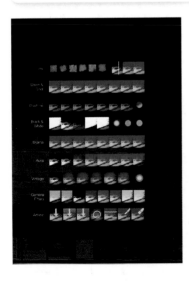

The final option is for adding effects. There are nine categories which each contain several different filter styles including vintage photos, colour palettes and even one that gives your picture the look of a watercolour painting. Touch the images at the bottom to change the filter or to change the category touch the icon second from the right at the bottom to access the main effect library.

Step 10: Sharing Your Photos

As you would expect, iPhoto has plenty of sharing options hidden under the boxed arrow icon including Facebook, Twitter, Flickr, email and more. You can also save your image to your Camera Roll here. Best of all though, is the Journal option. You can add a selection of images and iPhoto will compile them into a tasteful montage to keep the memories of the moment alive.

iPad Air

How To Use… Camera As A Video Recorder

The iPad is capable of recording high quality video footage that you can then enjoy on its big, beautiful screen. The video camera itself is pretty simple.

Step 1: Accessing The Video Recorder

Unlike most of the other features of your iPad, which all have their own individual apps, the video recorder functions aren't stand-alone. Instead, they're hidden inside the Camera app. If you open Camera and look to the lower-left hand side of the screen, you'll see three options – Video, Photo and Square. Photo will be highlighted by default. Swipe the list to highlight Video.

Step 2: Using The Video Recorder

Shooting video using the Camera app is simple. You just point your iPad at whatever you want to record and press the big red record button on the right. It'll keep recording until you press the button again. You can also use the volume buttons for this. Do be aware that video footage can take up a lot of storage space. If your iPad is full of other content, you might not have much room.

iTip – BE CAREFUL WHEN TRIMMING
If you pick Trim Original when editing your video down,
the full-length version will be deleted forever. Don't
do it unless you're absolutely sure you don't need it!

Step 3: Video Options

There aren't too many options to use while recording video with your iPad. You can touch the screen to choose a focal point or switch from the rear to front-side camera. The zoom function works in the same way as it does for the camera. Just pinch in and out and slide the marker on the bar for more delicate adjustments. You can do this in real time while you're shooting.

Step 4: Accessing Your Videos

When you've recorded a video, you'll find it waiting for you in your photo library. Just tap the small thumbnail image in the lower-right corner to access it. Tap the play button to play the video, then tap the screen again to bring up the controls that enable you to pause, delete it or share it via all the usual means. Tap the Done option at the top of the screen to return to the viewfinder view.

Step 5: Skipping And Sharing Videos

The bar at the top of the video is the timeline. You can touch this anywhere and drag your finger left or right to skip through the video to the bit you want. If you touch the arrow button at the bottom, you can share you video, and even upload it directly to YouTube if you have an account set up. Unfortunately, videos can't be shared via Photostream which only works with still images.

Step 6: Trimming Your Videos

If you want to trim your video down to get rid of unwanted bits, touch the left edge of the timeline until it's highlighted and drag it inwards to where you want the video to start. Repeat with the right edge for where it should end. Tap Trim and then select either Save To New File to create a new edited version or Trim Original to save over the old version.

iPad Air

iMovie

Price: £2.99
Developed By: Apple
In-app Purchases: No

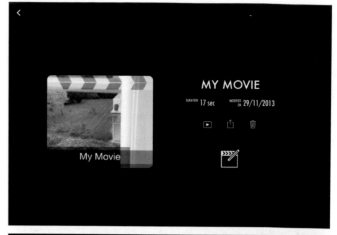

iMovie is the ultimate mobile video-editing app. Its powerful tool set will enable you to create professional-looking video projects on the go in just a few minutes.

It used to be that editing video footage captured on a camcorder was a time-consuming and expensive process. You needed the expensive camera kit itself, the gear needed to convert that footage into an editable format, and the skills to actually use the editing tools themselves.

Computers changed all that in terms of the kit needed and the fact that you could edit chunks of footage without the need to spool through it manually, but it was still expensive – in fact, it still can be. Apple's own Final Cut Pro X, possibly the most advanced video editing software available today, comes in at a whopping £200 and with good reason. It's used by professional video editors and has all the tools you could ever need. Quality video editing software isn't beyond the reach of the masses though, thanks to Apple packing many of the same tools from Final Cut into iMovie – a simpler, but still powerful editing suite that anyone can pick up and use.

You can get the Mac version of iMovie as part of the iLife package for a mere £40. Even better though, you can get the iPad version for the same price as a McDonald's breakfast, with the added bonus that it's far more satisfying when you're done with it. And best of all, the iPad app contains many of the functions offered by its big brother at a fraction of the price. The fact that it's entirely portable means you can record video and then immediately edit it down with effects and other tweaks before sharing it in a variety of ways on the fly, which is very cool indeed.

Despite being far more advanced than you'd expect a super-cheap mobile video-editing suite to be, the iPad version of iMovie is very easy to use thanks to its intuitive interface and simple drag-and-drop controls. Integration with the iPad's other apps like Camera and Photo Library means importing videos is simplicity itself – just tap, select and off you go. There's also the option to record videos straight into iMovie, then edit them immediately without even having to leave the app. If you've got videos on your

computer, you can also import those into iMovie through iTunes although they need to be the right format for iMovie to work with them.

You can share projects across multiple devices (iPhone, iPod Touch, iPad and Mac) through iTunes, meaning you can start editing a project on your iPad when you're out and about, then transfer to a Mac when you get home. The iOS version of the software is universal, so when you've paid for it once you can download it onto any other iOS devices you own for nothing.

The tool set of iMovie for iOS isn't as extensive as that of the Mac version but it's not all that far off. When you take into account both the price and the portability of the app, its value becomes very clear. Whether you're making family movies for posterity or putting together your own little creative projects, iMovie is a great way to dip your toes in the water of video editing. A truly excellent app and a must have for all iOS users.

How To Use... iMovie

iMovie is simple enough to use once you get the hang of it, but it's not entirely obvious how everything works the first time you fire it up. These steps will guide you through all the basic procedures you need to know.

Step 1: The Project Screen

When you first open iMovie, the only thing you'll be able to do is tap the plus button at the top to start a new movie project. In future, your created projects will appear on this screen for you to select from, complete with their names and length. To delete a project, highlight it by tapping it once then tap the bin icon to the bottom-right. Your project will then be gone for good.

Step 2: Using The Undo Feature

Before you import anything into your project, it's important that you know about a very crucial function of iMovie: the undo feature. If you make a mistake or do something wrong, you can immediately reverse it by shaking your iPad and pressing Undo. You can also do this to redo an action if you decide that you didn't want to undo what you undid after all.

Step 3: Adding Pre-Recorded Video

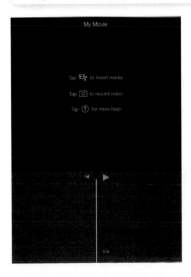

Once the timeline screen appears, tap the film/music icon at the upper right and you'll be taken to a library of all the videos currently stored on your iPad. To add one to your project, just tap it and tap the curly arrow button. You can also touch and drag the yellow markers on either end of each video snippet to add only the selected part of that video instead if you wish to do so.

Step 4: Recording Video In iMovie

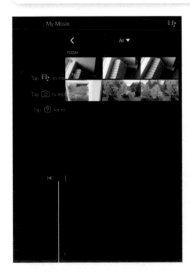

iMovie also gives you the option to record fresh video directly into the timeline. Tap the camera icon at the bottom and you'll get a similar display to the Camera app in video mode. After recording your video as normal, you can check it out using the play and timeline controls, then hit either Use to import it into your project or Retake to film a totally new video.

iPad Air

127

How To Use... iMovie (continued)

Step 5: Adding Photos To Your Project

Interestingly, you can also add stills photography to any iMovie project; perhaps you'll want to use one as a title screen or to help break up a particularly long scene. To do it, tap the film/music icon and then touch the photos button at the bottom of the page to reveal a similar interface to the Photos app. Tap the image you want to then insert it into your project's timeline.

Step 6: Rearranging Video/Photo Clips

Your video and photo content will appear on the timeline screen at the bottom, and you can keep adding clips/ photos until you've got everything you want to edit together. If you want to rearrange the clip/photo order, though, just touch and hold your finger on the one that you're moving, then drag it along the timeline to where you want it, before or after another clip.

Step 7: Advanced Clip Rearranging

If you want to reposition a clip/photo into the middle of a clip rather than the beginning or end, you need to create a split point. Drag the timeline at the bottom to exactly where you want the split to be and touch the clip to highlight it. Now swipe down with your finger quickly to cut the clip in half. This only works with video clips currently in the timeline, though, and not photos.

Step 8: Trimming Clip/Photo Length

Just as you did when you imported previously recorded video into your timeline, you can now trim down the length of your clips and photos by tapping the clip to highlight it, then dragging the yellow end markers inwards. The number shown indicating the clip length will decrease to compensate. When you're done, touch off the clip to deselect it and apply the trim.

iTip – SCOUTING YOUR LOCATION
When you first open iMovie, be sure to say OK if it asks to use your location data. If you don't, you won't be able to access videos or photos in your Camera Roll.

Step 9: Changing Project Settings

Tapping the cog button in the bottom right corner brings up the Project Settings menu. The main setting is the theme, which sets the style of any theme music or subtitles you apply. Simply drag the small windows left and right to pick the one you want. You can also turn on theme music here and set your project to fade to/from black at the start or the end of it.

Step 10: Playing With Transitions

Any breaks sitting between clips are handled by transitions. Double-tap one of the black squares between clips/photos to access the settings for that transition; you can choose its length and set the style to match your chosen theme, be it a simple cross-fade or nothing at all. Each transition is unique, so you need to change the settings for each one individually.

Step 11: Editing Photo Clips

Imported photos are different from video clips. Instead of playing, iMovie applies a movement effect called Ken Burns to make things more interesting. You can control this effect by tapping the photo, then dragging to change its position around and pinching to zoom in/out. Do this for the start and end to set positional markers and then iMovie fills in the blanks itself.

Step 12: Adding Captions And Locations

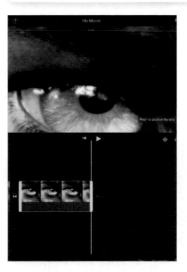

To add title captions to any clip, tap it to see the clip settings options appear across the bottom of the screen. Touch Title, choose where the caption will appear (at the start, middle or end), then tap the 'Title Text Here' box and fill in what you want it to say. To add a location, just tap Location, and tap the target button to detect your location or tap Other and type it in.

How To Use... iMovie (continued)

Step 13: Adjusting A Clip's Sound Levels

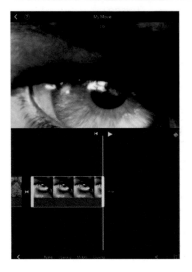

If you're currently viewing a video clip with sound attached, tap the audio option at the bottom left to display a volume control slider. You can slide this to the left or right with your finger to decrease or increase the sound level of the clip, or tap the speaker icon to mute or unmute the track. That's handy if you want a music track to take precedence (see step 14).

Step 14: Adding Your Own Music

Although you can apply generic music in the Project Settings screen, you can also add your own music track. Touch the film/music icon on the timeline screen, then tap Audio. Theme music and sound effects are provided by iMovie, while the other menus link to your music library. Just tap a song to add it to the timeline. You can adjust positioning and volume later.

Step 15: Changing Music Sound Levels

As with the clip settings of video clips and photos, you can tap any added music track (which appear under the image timeline as a thin green bar) to bring up the audio options. Obviously, the only thing you can change is the volume. Don't forget, added audio automatically fades when video audio is playing, unless you specifically set it not to do so.

Step 16: Deleting Clips And Audio

If you decide that you've added something that you now don't want, you can remove it by going into the clip settings for that section (tap the clip/photo/music track) and tapping the bin icon that appears at the bottom of the screen. Remember though, only do this if you're sure, because iMovie's undo option only undoes the last action performed, so be careful.

iTip – SPECIAL EFFECTS
You can use any video effect app available in the App Store to create video clips that work in iMovie, as long as the app outputs the video into your Camera Roll folder.

Step 17: Adding A Voiceover Track

To add a voiceover, move the timeline to where you want it to start, then press the microphone button at the bottom. Hit the record button when you're ready, watch the countdown, then start talking as the video plays. Hit Stop and review what you did, discard and re-record it or keep the track. Voiceovers appear in the timeline as purple bars to set them apart.

Step 18: Watching Your Edited Project

To see how your edited video is coming along, press the play button in the middle of the screen and it'll play from wherever you've set the timeline marker. Alternatively, press the back button in the top-left corner and then the play button on the Project screen to have it play from the start in full-screen mode (with the iPad in landscape mode), as you would a normal movie.

Step 19: Finalising Your Project

Once you're happy with your video project, it's time to finish it off. Start by giving it a proper title. Hit the back button in the top-left corner of the timeline screen to return to the Projects page, then tap the display where it says New Project. This brings up the keyboard, so type in a name for your video that describes it best and then hit the Done button to set it in place.

Step 20: Sharing Your Project

Now let's put your project where others can see it! Hit the arrow button at the bottom of the Projects screen to see iMovie's various sharing options; you can save it to your Camera Roll or upload it to YouTube or Facebook (if you have accounts logged in with your iPad) or even send it to iTunes, allowing you to pick up the project on an iPhone or iPod Touch if you have one.

iPad Air

131

How To Use… Green Screen Movie FX Studio

Green Screening enables film makers to mask the background in a video and to apply new backgrounds and special effects. With Green Screen Movie FX Studio, you can do exactly the same and get some amazing results.

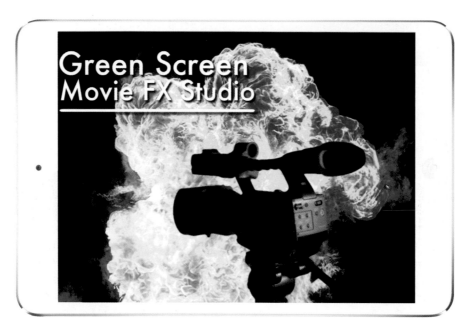

Step 1: So What Is Green Screen?

First you'll need to download the Green Screen Movie FX Studio app from the App Store. It enables you to place subjects against different backgrounds and add special effects in layers so it appears as though the subject is really there, in the middle of whatever crazy stuff is happening.

Step 2: The Subject

The first job is to shoot some footage of your subject. You need to film them against a single colour backdrop and they mustn't be wearing anything of the same colour. Bold colours such as bright blue or bright green work the best. When you're happy with your footage it's time to fire up the app.

iTip – TWEENING AND SCALING
If you want an effect to appear to come towards the foreground, use the tween option. This enables you to set both the position and size of the effect at its start and end.

Step 3: Create A Project

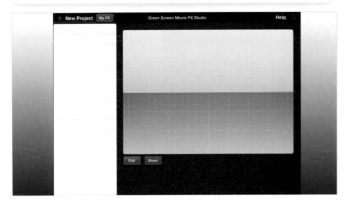

When the main screen appears, tap the New Project button at the top of the screen. You can then choose the video quality you want to produce – high quality takes longer to process. When you've made your selection you can choose to shoot a new video or import existing footage.

Step 4: Removing Colours

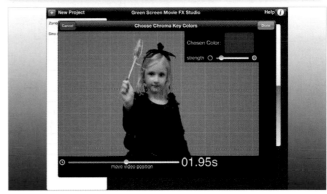

When you pull in your footage the first job is to remove the background. Tap on the background to select it as the chrome key in the box at the top right of the screen and all the corresponding colour will be removed from the footage. Adjust the level so that all noise is removed.

Step 5: Adding Effects

You can add effects to your video by tapping the Add Effect button. These are added in layers in the order they appear in the box. To re-order the layers, tap Move FX then drag them up or down the list. Typically you'll want the background at the bottom and the subject at the top.

Step 6: Fine Tuning

You can scale, drag and rotate all your layers until you have them perfectly positioned and when you're happy with everything tap Compose at the top of the screen. The video will then be processed, after which you can share it via all the usual means.

iPad Air

How To Use... Action Movie FX

Add amazing Hollywood movie-style special effects to your videos with
Action Movie FX and turn them all into massive blockbusters!

Step 1: Check out the FX

This app enables you to add proper special effects to your movies, from explosions to spaceships. When you first open it up you'll see all the various effects in a carousel. Swipe left and right to cycle through until you see one that takes your fancy. Then just tap on it to open up the preview window.

Step 2: Choose An Effect

When you select a clip you'll be taken to the preview window. You'll be able to see the effect in action in the small viewing pane and there are a few words of advice to help you maximise the impact of the effect that you're going to use. If you like the selected effect, tap the Start button.

iTip – LOOK OUT FOR NEW FX
Keep checking the app for new effects appearing in the store. It's regularly updated with awesome new additions for you to play around with.

Step 3: Shoot Your Video

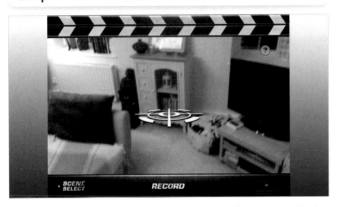

There will be a short loading time, then you'll get a viewfinder with a target in the centre and a record button at the bottom of the screen. Tap the record button and then aim the target where you want the special effect to hit. You can film as long as you want but you need to shoot at least five seconds.

Step 4: Add The FX

When you stop the recording you'll go to a new screen with a timeline and a red button marked FX. Drag this button along the timeline to the point where you want the effect to hit then tap OK to confirm. It will take a few seconds to process so be patient until you see the play button which means it's ready.

Step 5: Preview Your Video

Tap the play button and the clip will play complete with your special effect. If you're not happy with the timing of the effect, you can tap the back button to adjust it. If you're happy with it, tap the share button to post it to Facebook, email it or save it to your camera roll.

Step 6: Get More FX

The app itself is free and comes preloaded with some free effects, but there are more available to buy. Just scroll through the carousel to check them out. There's everything from crashing cars and falling wrecking balls to a flyby by the Starship Enterprise no less!

iPad Air

Photography and Video Apps

With the iPad's wonderful retina display it's no wonder that photography and video apps are so popular. Here are just a few that can help to add an extra little sprinkling of stardust to your snaps and vids.

Pixlr-o-matic

Price: Free
Developed By: Autodesk Inc
In-app Purchases: No

Autodesk is one of the biggest names in computer graphics software, so you know this app is going to be good. It offers over two million combinations of effects, filters, borders and overlays to create the perfect mood using your digital photos. It can give your pictures an extra dash of flair and style. Share them with your friends via the usual means.

Secret Photos KYMS

Price: Free
Developed By: IdeaSolutions S.r.l.
In-app Purchases: No

If you've got photos on your device that you'd rather other people didn't see, you can hide them using this clever little app. At first glance it appears to be a standard calculator app; it even works! But if you tap in your secret four-digit PIN it turns into a picture viewer and lets you see your hidden pictures. Ideal if you have any sensitive images on your iPad.

TagsForLikes

Price: Free
Developed By: Zaheer Mohiuddin
In-app Purchases: No

If you use Instagram then you'll know that the best way to get noticed is by using the right hashtags. It can be hard though, with so many people competing for attention. TagsForLikes makes it easy to quickly add frequently used hashtags to your pictures, essential if you regularly upload a large number of photos of fairly similar subject matter.

Adobe Revel

Price: Free
Developed By: Adobe
In-app Purchases: Yes

With Adobe Revel you can automatically sync your photos across your Mac, iPhone and iPad so you've always got access to your collection no matter where you are. Create albums, make quick touch-ups, add comments and share your photos using Facebook, Twitter or shared albums and more. It's another great option for sharing your images alongside the built-in ones.

ComicBook!

Price: £0.69
Developed By: 3DTOPO Inc
In-app Purchases: Yes

If you like to have fun with your photos, you should give this bargain-priced app a try. Turn your photos into instant comic books, with realistic art styles, a big range of page layouts and border styles, auto-scaling text captions with licensed comic text fonts, and lots of classic comic graphics. With a bit of practice you'll be able to create some really cool stuff and even come up with your own stories.

Drawcast

Price: Free
Developed By: Daniel Cota
In-app Purchases: No

Drawcast is part art package, part social network client, and part game. You can use your own images or import them, add your own unique drawings using layers, upload the results to Facebook, and even capture video of you creating your masterpiece. It has cool drawing tools, plus a colour mixer. It's one of those apps that you really have to try out for yourself.

Adobe Photoshop Touch

Price: £2.99
Developed By: Adobe
In-app Purchases: No

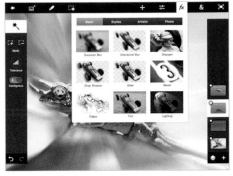

There's one name that has been associated with digital photo editing since time immemorial, and that name is Photoshop. Adobe's photo editor has always been the professional's choice for good reason – it's the best software of its kind available. These days, with powerful digital cameras in our phones, we're all amateur photographers. If you want to make more of your photos then you'll be pleased to find out (if you didn't know already) that an iOS version of Photoshop is available that will enable you to edit your images on the move, right on your iPad. Naturally it's nothing like the professional desktop version, but who would want that on the iPad anyway? What you get is still a powerful and feature-packed editing app that enables you to resize images, add all kinds of effects, use brushes and lots more. As apps go, it's on the pricey side and if you don't ever plan to do anything more than basic photo-editing then you may want to opt for a free alternative. If you're looking for more features and flexibility though, then Photoshop Touch is for you. This is easily among the top digital image editing apps available in the App Store.

JustSeen

Price: Free
Developed By: JustSeen.com Ltd.
In-app Purchases: No

Photo-based social networking apps are very popular with services such as Instagram, Tumblr and Snapchat achieving massive success, not to mention photo sharing via Facebook and the ubiquitous Twitter. Apparently there's room for one more though, because here we have JustSeen, an app that lets you instantly send and view photos live from anywhere in the world. Photos are organised by category, location and keyword, and like other networks you can have friends and followers. Only time will tell if it will catch on, but it's good.

PureShot

Price: £1.49
Developed By: Michael Hardaker
In-app Purchases: No

While funky filters and effects are great for casual snapshots, no serious photographer would be caught dead using them. Of course no pro photographer would normally use an iPad camera, but if they did they'd use PureShot. It captures the highest quality that the iPad camera can produce, including a super high-quality dRAW TIFF format similar to images produced by top-end cameras. With other great features like spot metering, exposure histogram and bracketing and many more, this app can revolutionise your iPad photography.

Picmatic

Price: Free
Developed By: Team Whiskey Beavers
In-app Purchases: No

If your iPad is sitting on your desk doing nothing some of the time, why not use it as a digital picture frame? Picmatic from Team Whiskey Beavers is a great app that can do just that, as well as playing music and even telling you the time. With a huge range of layouts, dozens of filters that you can apply to your pics, and loads of cool transition effects, your pictures will never have looked better, and the smart gesture control lets you tap anywhere on the screen to play music, or swipe through to select new tunes. A cool way to use your iPad when you're not using it!

Photography and Video Apps (continued)

Videolicious

Price: Free
Developed By: The Talk Market
In-app Purchases: No

Ever wanted to make a great video clip but don't have a clue where to start? Videolicious does much of the work for you! Just choose the clips you want to include in your video, put them in order and add some music, then the app builds a professional-looking video package automatically with no effort on your part. You can still claim all the credit though.

MoviePro

Price: £1.99
Developed By: Mirage Labs Private Ltd
In-app Purchases: No

MoviePro is great for budding amateur film makers and offers a host of features to help you record better footage and get the effects you want. You can select different frame rates and resolutions, it supports landscape and portrait mode and boasts lots more great elements to make your movies even better. Not cheap, but well worth the price.

Backwards Cam

Price: £1.49
Developed By: Zihae
In-app Purchases: No

This app does exactly what the title suggests – it enables you to shoot footage then watch it in reverse to create hilarious backwards movies. It's a great bit of fun and can be used to make even the most mundane movements and actions a source of amusement. The price is a bit on the steep side but if you can afford it, it's good fun.

Video Star

Price: Free
Developed By: Frontier Design Group
In-app Purchases: Yes

Have you ever fancied starring in your very own music video? Now you can, thanks to this super fun app. Play your favourite song, mime along and add all manner of effects to make the most awesome video possible. Lots of extra effects are available as in-app purchases which just make it even better. This is sure to go down well with anyone who loves The X-Factor. Tons of fun.

Videon

Price: £1.99
Developed By: Lucky Clan
In-app Purchases: No

If you want a one stop shop video app that does everything from shoot to edit, then you might want to check out Videon. The emphasis is on simplicity, but it has some cool features such as a zoom function. The interface is nice and chunky and it all works pretty well. It's a jack of all trades and a pretty good one at that. Just don't expect the level of control you get in iMovie.

VideoGrade

Price: £2.99
Developed By: Fidel Lainez
In-app Purchases: No

This app enables you to enhance the look of your videos through adjusting colour gradients and adding various filters and effects. With practice you can obtain all kinds of cool looks and effects that will add a great deal of interest and stylistic value to your movies. A really cool app that iOS movie makers should really consider. Try it in conjunction with some of our featured apps for great results.

8mm for iPad

Price: £1.49
Developed By: Nexvio Inc
In-app Purchases: No

The large screen coupled with its video-capture capability make the iPad an ideal platform for amateur movie-makers as well as anyone who wants to capture treasured moments forever. 8mm is a simple but fantastic app that enables you to add various retro-themed filters and textures to your video footage in real-time to give it the look of old film stock from various different eras. You can go for the gritty look of the 70s where you'll half expect Clint Eastwood to step into shot, Magnum in hand, at any moment. You can go back further with the sixties filter for that summer of love vibe. If that's still a bit too 'now' for you, you can go right back to the silent movies of the 20s. All the filters work really well and look thoroughly authentic when you play them back. You can even add the sound effect of an old-style movie projector rattling away in the background for added ambience. You can also drop in spooling glitches to really give the impression of watching vintage footage.

If you want an app that can make every one of your videos unique without even having to touch an editor, this is it. Try it. You won't be disappointed.

Pro HDR

Price: £1.49
Developed By: eyeApps LLC
In-app Purchases: No

This clever and cheap app enables you to really maximise your photography with little fuss. Pro HDR, as with the HDR (which stands for High Dynamic Range) option that you'll find in the iPad camera app, actually takes multiple photos at the same time, each one tuned to a specific element: highlights, shadows and so on. It then merges these photos together to capture the best of each element and helps you get a photo that really represents what you can see, rather than losing things like sky or foreground through a lack or excess of light.

VideoCam3D Lite

Price: Free
Developed By: NXP Software
In-app Purchases: No

The world of 3D video has come a long way in recent times thanks to handheld devices like the Nintendo 3DS, but there's still room for old-fashioned 3D effects too. Unlike new technology that allows you to see 3D without the need for glasses, VideoCam3D uses good old red and blue filters to separate video footage before letting you play it back in 3D – provided you have a pair of old-school 3D glasses to hand, that is. Not only can it record fresh video with the effect, but it can also be used to apply 3D effects retrospectively to videos that you've already recorded.

Video Editor for FREE

Price: Free
Developed By: From the Top
In-app Purchases: No

We've got a complete tutorial on Apple's iMovie video editor earlier in this section, but if that's a bit too expensive or complicated for you then this cheap and cheerful alternative will enable you to cut, edit and splice your video footage together very simply. Obviously it doesn't have the power or options of iMovie but if you just want to be able create family movies quickly and easily then look no further. You can create movies of up to ten minutes in length which is plenty for most occasions and it doesn't cost a penny.

Your iPad Air And
Organisation

The iPad Air can be used to organise your entire life. It comes with several essential apps designed to help in all aspects of your day-to-day existence from doing the chores to remembering dates and appointments. Calendar doesn't need too much more explanation; you can enter events, details, add reminders, sync up with calendars on other devices and share your calendars with others to ensure you never double-book. We have a tutorial that explains how to get the most out of Calendar and how to utilise its deeper functionality.

The clock app enables you to set up multiple alarms so your iPad can let you know when important events are about to begin. There's also an app called Reminders that can become your daily task manager. Enter the jobs you need to do and check them off as you complete them. Simple. All these features are fully explained in our simple step-by-step guides, and we have recommendations of more excellent organisational apps for you as well.

"[The iPad] comes with several essential apps to help in all aspects of your day-to-day existence from doing the chores to remembering dates and appointments"

142 How To Use Reminders

- Create A Reminder
- Make A List
- Set A Date
- Get A Regular Reminder
- Prioritise Reminders
- Feel A Sense of Accomplishment

144 How To Use Calendar

- Viewing Forthcoming Events
- Adding Events
- Naming Events
- Setting A Time For Your Event
- Repeated Events
- Event Reminders

146 How To Use Notification Center

- Where Is Notification Center?
- Changing Notification Settings
- Turning Notifications On/Off
- Leave Me Alone

147 How To Use Dictation

- Talk To Siri
- Make A Note
- Send Tweets, Emails, And More
- Check What You're Sending

148 Organisation Apps

- Budget Sheet Manager
- EasyDiscount
- Evernote
- Dropbox
- MyCalendar Mobile
- Remember The Milk
- Shopping List Free
- 30/30
- CamScanner HD Pro
- iPlanner HD

How To Use... Reminders

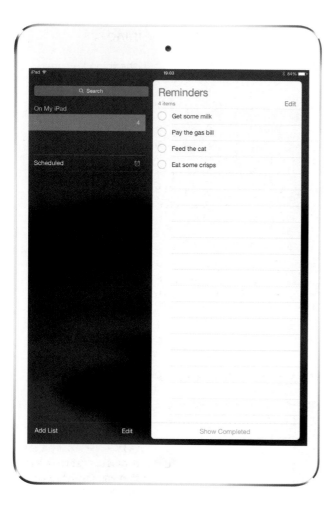

Reminders is a handy and completely customisable checklist that will ensure you never again forget any of those important things you need to do.

Step 1: Create A Reminder

The Reminders app is pre-loaded on your iPad and appears on your home screen. Touch it to open it and you'll see a blank list. However, if you want to become super-organised, that list won't stay blank for long! Tap one of the lines to create your first reminder. The keyboard will appear and you can just type in whatever it is you need to remember to do. Don't worry about being too descriptive.

Step 2: Make A List

If you think you'll remember to check your reminders list regularly enough, that's all you need to do. You can just keep typing in your to-do list, save it, and refer back to it whenever necessary. However, the point of a reminder is to actually remind you. With that in mind, once you've entered your task, touch it then tap the blue information icon that appears. This opens the Details box.

iPad Air

142

Step 3: Set A Date

In the Details box that pops up, touch the slider next to Remind Me On A Day and you can set a timed reminder. So if you need to remember to buy milk before your mum comes round, use the date sliders to enter a date and time. This can be as soon or as far in the future as you like. If there's no deadline, then you can just skip this step.

Step 4: Get A Regular Reminder

If the thing you need to remember is a recurring event, such as an appointment or a birthday or perhaps a gym class, then you can use the Repeat function in the Reminders menu so you don't have to keep entering it time after time. That way, your iPad will remind you every time this task is due. This is particularly helpful for anniversaries which you really don't want to forget!

Step 5: Prioritise Reminders

When you have a long list of things that need doing, it can be hard to know where to start, but the Reminders app will let you assign each task a priority level. There are four levels of priority if you count the first level as none. The three buttons containing one, two and three exclamation marks respectively enable you to apply a suitable priority level to the selected reminder.

Step 6: Feel A Sense of Accomplishment

When you've completed a task on your list, you just need to touch the box next to it on the Reminders list to tick it off. If you tap where it says Show Completed you'll see all tasks you've completed while you've been using Reminders, and to hide them again, tap Hide Completed. Effective use of Reminders is a great way to organise your life and you'll wonder how you managed without it.

iPad Air

How To Use... Calendar

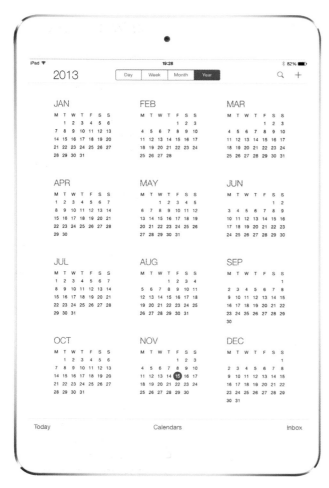

Calendar needs no introduction. You know what it's all about. The iOS 7 version has a cool new look and it makes the whole thing clearer and easier to use than ever.

Step 1: Viewing Forthcoming Events

Once you're in the Calendar app, you'll see that there are a number of choices about how you can view your upcoming plans – daily, monthly or as a list (shown here). The month view shows a dot beneath any day upon which you have an event scheduled, while the daily view breaks it into half-hour chunks. The list, meanwhile, shows all your appointments in date order.

Step 2: Adding Events

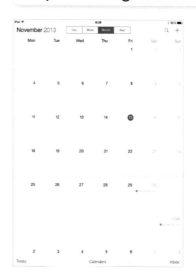

In the month view, you can move forward and back through the months by swiping up and down. The current date is highlighted. Touch and hold a day to bring up the option to add an event on that day. After a moment the New Event panel will open where you can enter details for your event, or you can back out without adding an event by tapping the Cancel option.

Step 3: Naming Events

You can now name your event to remind you what it is and you can also enter the location where it'll take place in. Whatever you type into the top box will be the name of the event and is what will be displayed in your info box (should you set a reminder) and in the calendar, so you should make the name self-explanatory. After all, you want to be able to tell what things are at a glance.

Step 4: Setting A Time For Your Event

The box below enables you to set exactly when the event will be happening. By default, the date will match the one highlighted in your diary, but you can use the scroll wheels to change this, as well as setting a start and end time for your appointment. You can change the date on the end time if an event runs over more than one day, and the slider can indicate an all-day event.

Step 5: Repeated Events

It may be that you have a recurring event and you don't want to have to enter it separately every time it occurs. Selecting the Repeat box gives you some pre-set repeat options for dealing with frequent events. Note that monthly repeats the meeting on the same date each month, rather than, for example, on the first Monday and the same applies for the yearly settings as well.

Step 6: Event Reminders

You can tell Calendar how much notice you want prior to the event by selecting the Alert box. You can choose to be reminded of your meeting either as it's due to start or at different intervals beforehand. You can also set a second reminder nearer the time. You can save your reminder(s) for just this event or all instances if it's a recurring one.

iPad Air

How To Use... Notification Center

Through Notification Center, your iPad keeps you up to date with everything you need to know from new posts on Facebook to emails and app updates. It's your at-a-glance guide to all the things you need to be aware of.

Step 1: Where Is Notification Center?

Opening Notification Center is very easy. Swiping your finger down from the top of the screen brings it up instantly, no matter whether you're on the home screen or in an app. Notification Center is only ever one swipe away with this simple gesture. To close it down, just repeat the gesture in reverse, (swiping up from the bottom of the screen) and it will disappear.

Step 2: Changing Notification Settings

So, how do we determine which apps are displayed in the Notification Center? It gives you immediate access to the latest updates from apps that you have selected, so only choose the most relevant apps. You can start that process by touching the Settings menu and then choosing Notification Center to bring up a list. Then just enable or disable apps as required.

Step 3: Turning Notifications On/Off

Touch any of the items in the list and you'll be able to toggle notifications on and off. You can also set more detailed instructions. For example, you can choose how many updates from a specific app should be shown in the Notifications panel, whether info should appear as a banner, an alert or not at all, and whether they should appear on the lock screen or not.

Step 4: Leave Me Alone

If you want to temporarily disable everything, you can set your iPad to Do Not Disturb mode. This will silence all incoming alerts until you manually disengage it. You can find the Do Not Disturb option in the Settings menu under Notification Center and Control Center. The importance of setting up Notification Center properly shouldn't be underestimated.

How To Use... Dictation

If you need to take a note, send a tweet or message, or jot something down, you can get Siri to do it for you.
All you need to know are a few basic commands so Siri knows what it is you want to do.

Step 1: Talk To Siri

You probably turned Siri on when you were setting up your iPad, but just in case you didn't, you can easily do it now. Open the Settings menu, touch General, and then tap Siri and toggle the switch to On. Now, to get started talking to Siri, press and hold the home button on your iPad, and Siri will pop up in a new window to ask what it can help with.

Step 2: Make A Note

Siri can take dictation of pretty much anything you'd normally type – you just have to ask. Touch the microphone and ask Siri to take a new note by saying "Take a note." Siri will respond by asking what you want the note to say, then just say whatever it is you want the note to say. It's really that simple. If you want to add punctuation, you can just say it as you go along.

Step 3: Send Tweets, Emails And More

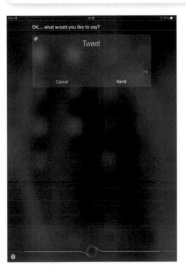

It's not just notes you can get Siri to take down for you. You can also ask it to send a tweet, email or message. Depending on what you're sending, you may need to add a recipient or a subject line, but Siri will ask you for that information as you go along You just need to tap the microphone button before replying to make sure that Siri is actually listening.

Step 4: Check What You're Sending

Siri is pretty good at understanding dictation, but it isn't always perfect, especially when it comes to words that sound identical, like 'whether' and 'weather.' Before sending anything, you should probably take a moment to check and correct anything that Siri has written for you to avoid any potentially embarrassing misunderstandings.

Organisation Apps

One sure way to make your life easier is to get organised. Your iPad can help you to do just that in many ways thanks to a wide range of organisational apps geared for everything you can think of.

Budget Sheet Manager

Price: £0.69
Developed By: V Lokeswara Reddy
In-app Purchases: No

With austerity biting hard for most people, it's never been more important to keep a tight rein on your budget, and that's where this app can really help. It provides useful features to help you manage your income and expenses. You can group your expenses into categories, set yourself a budget and track it all.

EasyDiscount

Price: £0.69
Developed By: Elliott Garage
In-app Purchases: No

This app gives you a fast, easy and efficient shopping calculator to check prices and discounts when you're out shopping. It can keep running totals, store multiple tax percentages and work out how much you're spending and saving on the fly while you shop. It's nicely presented and easy to use, so buy it now and start saving. It really does work.

Evernote

Price: Free
Developed By: Evernote
In-app Purchases: Yes

When it comes to organisation, Evernote is one of the most powerful tools available, helping you to retrieve relevant information quickly and easily while being ridiculously simple to use. Evernote allows you to save notes as images, text, web clippings and audio files. You can tag them as you see fit and access them from anywhere.

Dropbox

Price: Free
Developed By: Dropbox
In-app Purchases: yes

Dropbox enables you to store folders in an online space and work across different computers (like home and work). This app allows you to access, upload and download files on the move, meaning you can work on your files wherever you are. You'll need to install it on your computer as well though to make the most of it. It's a great tool.

MyCalendar Mobile

Price: £0.69
Developed By: K-Factor Media
In-app Purchases: No

We love the new iOS 7 calendar app but if it doesn't work for you then you might like to check out this great alternative. The chunky look gives it a really friendly feel and it comes with all the features you could possibly need. A very nice all round calendar that even gives the official Apple app a good run for its money. If you're looking for a quality alternative, look no further.

Remember The Milk

Price: Free
Developed By: Remember The Milk
In-app Purchases: Yes

This feature-packed app is also a complete life-saver, an organiser that can really help you to run your life and ensure that you never forget anything ever again, including the milk. It links to a subscription service which will remind you via email or instant message about anything you need to remember. A very useful app that anyone can make use of.

Shopping List Free

Price: Free
Developed By: hensoft
In-app Purchases: No

There are some things in life that just can't be avoided. Usually they are the less fun things, but your iPad can help to make some of them a little easier. One such thing is shopping. How often do you walk back in the door after a trip to the supermarket only to realise you forgot the most important thing that you went out to buy? It's easy to forget things even when you make a list and so annoying when it happens. Shopping List Free will put an end to that. Not only does it mean an end to scribbling lists down on the backs of old envelopes or any other bit of scrap paper that comes to hand, but it also enables you to save your lists, quantities and so on. You can even organise your lists into product categories so you can see at a glance if there's anything you need that you haven't added. The ability to store shopping lists means you'll never forget the essentials and all you have to add are any extra items you don't normally buy.

Shopping List Free is simplicity itself to use. It doesn't do anything wild or crazy, but it does exactly what it sets out to do perfectly. Never forget a vital ingredient again with this simple but invaluable app.

30/30

Price: Free
Developed By: Binary Hammer
In-app Purchases: Yes

Simple but incredibly effective, 30/30 is a task manager that has won multiple awards and been featured on TV. It's very easy to use; simply set up a list of tasks, allocate a length of time for each task on the list, and then when you start the timer, the app will tell you when to move on to the next task. You can control the task list with gestures, which feels natural and intuitive, and lists can sync over iCloud. The basic app is free, with extra icon packs available as in-app purchases. A great way to help you organise your time when multi-tasking.

CamScanner HD Pro

Price: £2.99
Developed By: IntSig Information Co Ltd
In-app Purchases: Yes

There are a number of document scanner apps available on the App Store, but few can match CamScanner HD for features, performance and quality. With CamScanner HD on your iOS device, simply use the rear camera to take a picture of any paper documents, such as files, receipts, whiteboards, etc. You can preview the picture on screen, save the best result or re-scan it and CamScanner will convert the photo to an industry-standard PDF file. It can even detect the document edges and remove the image background.

iPlanner HD

Price: £0.69
Developed By: David Pejinovic
In-app Purchases: No

A good organiser app is essential for anyone who uses their iOS device for business or to help organise their life. iPlanner HD is one of the best organisers on the App Store, and reasonably priced too. It offers a clear and simple user interface with national holidays, weekends and today's date clearly marked. You can mark and categorise your events with colour backgrounds or easily recognisable icons, and view your calendars by week, month or year. iPlanner supports AirPrint and can output calendars in PDF format.

iPad Air

Your iPad Air And
Communication

The iPad is a tool for communication through a wide range of apps, channels and media, and in this section we'll guide you through all of it's built-in communication options. Messages is a fully functioning instant messenger service. It's free to use to communicate with other iOS devices and enables users to chat, share files and more. We'll also guide you though setting up your email accounts to be accessible on your iPad. You can add as many as you want, so you can keep in touch with all your personal and work emails at all times.

The iOS 7 operating system features full Twitter and Facebook integration. You can Tweet or Facebook from most apps with just a couple of touches. We take you through signing in and also how to use the official Twitter and Facebook apps (available from the App Store). We've also got a selection of the best third party communication and social networking apps for you, covering everything from chatting to finding a date. It's time to get social!

> "The iOS 7 operating system features full Twitter and Facebook integration. You can Tweet or Facebook from most apps with just a couple of touches"

152 How To Use Messages

- Your Inbox
- Adding Recipients
- Adding Text And Sending Messages
- Predictive Text And Corrections
- Adding Photos And Videos
- Deleting Messages

iPad Air

How To Use... Messages

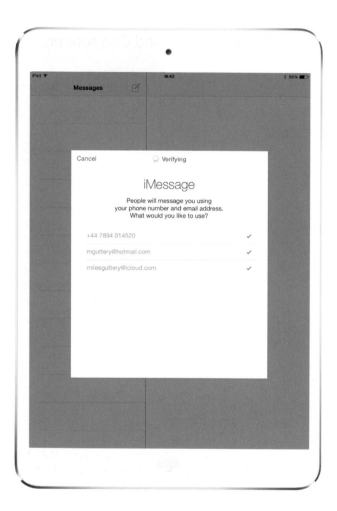

iMessages is Apple's sleek and powerful instant messaging app. Message any other iOS device for free, chat, exchange files and more.

Step 1: Your Inbox

Open the Messages app to see an empty screen with 'Messages' at the top. This is where all your conversations will eventually be stored. Of course, it'll be empty if you haven't used your iPad to send any messages before. The small pen and paper button at the top of the screen opens up a blank new message window. Tap this now to start writing your first iMessage right away.

Step 2: Adding Recipients

Touch the To field and use the keyboard to enter the number of the person to whom you want to send the message. If their details are already in your contact list, type the first few letters of their name to automatically bring up the names and numbers of people that match. Press the plus (+) button to bring up your contact list and select recipients that way if you prefer.

iTip – APPLE FRIENDS

iMessages only allows you to communicate with other Apple device users. To chat with non-Apple users you'll need a third party chat app such as WhatsApp.

Step 3: Adding Text And Sending Messages

Now tap the text field just above the keyboard to start entering your message text. The iPad has no character limit on text messages, so don't worry about running out of space – you can write as much as you like. When you're done and you've added all the desired recipients, simply hit Send to send your message and store a copy in your message library for future reference if required.

Step 4: Predictive Text And Corrections

The iPad loves predictive text and grammar correction, so don't be surprised when it tries to pre-empt or correct words, or check your text when you're done to make sure it's right! If there's an error, touch and hold down on a word to select and correct it. Touching and holding on a word also enables you to find suggested words or get a dictionary definition of a word.

Step 5: Adding Photos And Videos

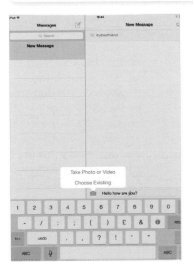

To add a photo or video, tap the camera button on the left. You'll get the option to take a photo or video immediately (refer to pages 116 and 124 for more on doing that) or add one from your Camera Roll or Photo Stream. Do be aware, though, that large files will take a long time to send, so trying to send someone a long video may not be worth your time or theirs. Keep that in mind.

Step 6: Deleting Messages

If you use iMessage a lot you might find that your inbox gets pretty cluttered. Luckily there's a quick way to delete threads. Just tap the Edit button on the upper-left side of the screen and red buttons will appear beside each conversation. Touch one and a Delete button will magically appear. Just press it to erase the conversation from your iPad. Note this action can't be undone.

iPad Air

How To Use... FaceTime

Video call for free with anybody you know that owns an iOS device or Mac. Follow these simple steps to get FaceTime up and running.

Step 1: FaceTime On Your iPad

FaceTime is built into the Phone app on an iPhone, but on the iPad it's a separate app. You'll find the icon on your home screen (or possibly in a folder, if you've tidied it away!). To get started making a call, just touch the icon. Note, though, that it works best with a Wi-Fi connection. Due to the data required, 3G and 4G performance can be choppy. Give it a try if you want though.

Step 2: Limitations Of FaceTime

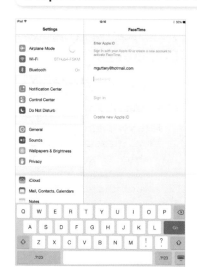

The other limitation to be aware of before you get started, is that the person you're calling will also need to have their own iOS device with FaceTime and Wi-Fi or a good quality 3G/4G connection. This means FaceTime calls are best arranged in advance to ensure that both people are able to connect. This might sound like quite a hassle, but being able to see who you're talking to makes it worth the effort.

iTip – 3G/4G FACETIME
You can make FaceTime calls on your 3G/4G network, but do beware that it can gobble up lots of your data allowance.

Step 3: Using FaceTime

In order to make a FaceTime call, you'll need to set FaceTime up with your email address. Go into Settings and choose FaceTime, make sure the FaceTime option is on and the Apple ID is correct, then enter an email address as your contact info for FaceTime. Give this to people you want to FaceTime with and store their details in your contacts list. Now pick a person to call.

Step 4: Get Connected

Open the FaceTime app and you'll see a list of all your contacts. Touch any of the names and you'll open a tab of information about them which includes their contact details and all the different ways you can contact them. Hit the camera icon to make a FaceTime call. If they're available, you'll soon see their face appear on your screen. Do remember that they can see you too!

Step 5: In-Call Controls

While you're in a FaceTime call, you'll see your own face in a smaller box in the corner. That little box lets you see what the other person is seeing, so you can make sure you keep that heap of laundry out of the shot! By default, FaceTime uses the front camera, but you can swap to the back camera by touching the flip icon. There's also an option to mute your mic.

Step 6: Ending A Call

Now you're connected, you can chat to your heart's content. Video calls may never have become as popular as sci-fi predicted, but if you're talking to far away friends, it's great to be able to see them and their surroundings! Stay within reach of your Wi-Fi connection, though, or you may find your call will disconnect. To hang up, just hit the End button and that, as they say, is that.

iPad Air

How To Use... Mail

You can sync up all your email accounts to be accessible on your iPad at all times. Follow these steps to get Mail working for you.

Step 1: Choose A Mail Provider

Interestingly, Apple has made the iPad's Mail app as all-encompassing as possible by making it compatible with a huge number of email services including Gmail, Microsoft Exchange, Yahoo!, Hotmail and more. You need to already have a suitable email account first, because only Apple's iCloud service lets you sign up directly through the iPad.

Step 2: Account Setup

Go to the Settings menu and select Mail, Contacts, Calendars, then choose Add Account. Pick your service provider from the fairly extensive list provided and then enter your login details for that account. Once the iPad has verified your information, it'll sync up with your mail server and will be ready to go. You can then add more email accounts – as many as you like, in fact!

Step 3: Other Service Providers

Of course, it may be you're using an email provider that isn't listed on your iPad by default. In that case, scroll to the bottom of the list and pick Other. Tap Add Mail Account and then enter your login details for the account as before. Mail works with most POP and IMAP-based mail servers, but check with your service provider if you can't get it to work and they should be able to help.

Step 4: Tweak Your Settings – Push

First, let's play with the email settings. Select Mail, Contacts, Calendars from the Settings menu, then touch Fetch New Data. Ideally, you want Push to be turned on, as this makes your mail server push new emails to your iPad as they arrive in your server inbox. If you're going away though, you should remember to turn it off to help keep your phone bills down.

Step 5: Tweak Your Settings – Mail

The next batch of settings, under the heading Mail, are all about personal preference. Increasing the number of emails to store on your phone, reducing the font size, sending yourself copies of mail – it's all to be found here. You can also change the signature sent with all emails, since the default signature gives away that you're mailing from your iPad.

Step 6: Tweak Your Settings – Accounts

Finally, scroll to the top and touch your email account under Accounts for one last setting. Archive Messages enables you to either permanently delete or save emails to your All Mail folder from your iPad with the on/off switch. Remember, though: delete means delete! Be absolutely sure before you set it to remove your emails for good as you won't be able to get them back.

iPad Air

How To Use... Mail (continued)

Step 7: View Your Account – Multiple

When you actually open the Mail app, what you see depends on what you've already set up. The screen shown here on the left is based on an iPad with multiple email accounts working on it. You can opt to view all the inboxes at once, view them separately or see a detailed version of each account. If you only have one email account, you'll see a screen like the one in the next step.

Step 8: View Your Account – Single

And here it is. As you can see, it's a pretty similar but more detailed display of your account. Multi-account users can access this by going into the Accounts panel. From here, you can see everything: your inbox, any half-written drafts, emails sent and anything that's been moved to one of the various labelled folders. Simply touch any folder to open it up and see the contents.

Step 9: View Your Inbox

Touching Inbox shows you a list of emails currently in your inbox. Unread emails will have a blue marker by them on the left. Multiple emails in the same chain are indicated by a number on the right, denoting the number of messages in the exchange. If you touch the single email shown in the inbox, you'll open another page showing you all the emails in the conversation.

Step 10: Searching Mail

To search for a specific email, touch the search bar at the top and type something such as a name or a keyword, using the From/To/Subject/All buttons to specify what part of the email the search relates to. Anything relevant in your inbox will be shown in a list. If it's not on your phone, touch Continue Search On Server to search your mail server and find a match. If it's there, you'll find it.

Step 11: Read, Delete And Archive Emails

To open an email, touch it and then drag up or down with your finger to scroll through it; you can also use the pinch motion to zoom in/out. The middle three buttons on the blue bar at the bottom are shortcuts – use them to save the email to a folder, delete/archive it (depending on the settings you chose earlier on) or send a reply to one or all of the people on the email.

Step 12: Contact Details

If you touch one of the blue email addresses at the top of any email, you can expand the name into a contact page. You can then save the email address to your contacts, either as a completely new contact or as an addition to one you already have. If it's already linked to a contact, you can send that person messages, or Facetime them instead. what ever works for you.

Step 13: Email Recipients

Press the pencil button in the top-right corner of the screen and you'll get the New Message template. To add a recipient, either touch the plus button to see your contacts or type the name in directly. If you've sent emails from your iPad before, then a list of names will appear matching the letters that you type. You can add as many names to an email chain as you like.

Step 14: Sending Emails

Entering text into the subject header and email body is simply a matter of touching the screen to move the cursor and then typing. To quickly correct or delete anything you've just typed, tap it to select it. When you're done, just touch the Send button to send it or you can press Cancel and either save what you've written already as a draft or discard it completely.

iPad Air

159

How To Use... Twitter

Twitter is the ultimate communication tool, enabling users to debate the big issues of the day, chat with celebrities and share amusing pictures!

Step 1: Downloading The Twitter App

You can search for the official Twitter app in the App Store if you like, but it's far simpler just to choose Twitter from the Settings menu and then hit the Install button at the top of the page. The app will then be installed just as if you'd downloaded it from the App Store. You can sign in on the Settings menu and it will then automatically sign you into the app when you start it up.

Step 2: Setting Up Your Account

If you're already signed up to Twitter and you have connected through iOS 7, you should be logged in automatically. If not, you'll need to add your account details now, so tap the plus button and fill in your username and password. When you press Save, you will be logged in and your details will be remembered next time you open the app, unless you sign out manually.

iTip – TWITTER AND iOS 7
Twitter is fully integrated into iOS 7 so you don't have to open the app to post and share stuff. Just select Twitter from the sharing options where available.

Step 3: Using The Twitter Feed

You will now be taken to the Twitter home page. The feed displayed here will show you all the updates from all the people you follow. You can click on individual tweets to copy, reply, retweet or otherwise share them. Selecting the name of the person who posted a message will bring up the full profile of that member for you to check out, much the same as in the browser version.

Step 4: Know Your Pages

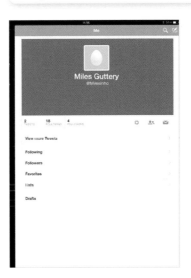

You can see your own profile, from which you can send personal messages, by pressing Me at the bottom of the screen. Connect shows replies to your tweets, tweets containing your username and who is following you. Tapping Discover will show you popular topics from the wider Twitter community that correspond to things mentioned in your own Twitter feed.

Step 5: Sending A Tweet

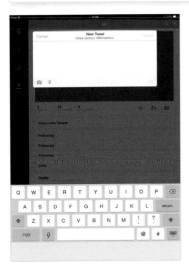

In the top right hand corner of the screen there's a button displaying a quill pen in a square. Tap this in order to compose a new tweet. When you do so, the keyboard interface will pop up allowing you to type out your message, and as soon as you press the Tweet button at the top, it will be propelled into the ether for all your followers to read. Simple as you like.

Step 6: Added Extras

When you're mentioning other people in a tweet, press the @ button and tap the name in the list that appears, or you can type it out longhand if you prefer. You can add pictures or a location to your tweet by pressing the camera and arrow buttons, for hashtags, type # and pick from the list or enter it manually as above. Look for the Twitter option whenever you share anything to tweet it instantly.

How To Use... Facebook

You can post to Facebook via iOS 7 integration but to see what your friends are up to, you need to download the official app. Here's how it works.

Step 1: Download Facebook

Facebook, you may or may not be aware, is fully integrated into iOS 7. To access it, go into Settings and scroll down until you see the Facebook option. Tap on it and you'll be prompted to enter your login details. You can also download the app from here. You don't need the app to share stuff but you will need it if you want to interact in any other way. You'll need your log in details.

Step 2: The News Feed

If you haven't used the iOS version of Facebook for a little while you may notice that things have changed slightly. It's basically the same but the navigation tools have been moved around. The default main view will be your news feed with the latest entries at the top. You can scroll up and down using your finger to see older updates just as you'd expect. There's no pinch to zoom though.

iTip – FACEBOOK CHAT
When you're chatting with someone on Facebook you'll see a little floating bubble with their profile pic in it. To get rid of it, drag it down to the white circle with a red 'X' in it.

Step 3: Update Your Status

Above the news feed are three tabs, the function of which should be pretty clear. The left most is Status. Tap on this to bring up the keyboard and text field in order to update your Facebook status. The middle option enables you to add a picture from your stored images. The final option is Check In which enables you to tag your location using GPS.

Step 4: Update The News Feed

The news feed shows all the most recent entries. To see more, scroll right to the bottom then wait a few moments and older posts will be loaded in. You can see posts as far back as you want to go. If you tap the bar at the top which says News Feed on it you can choose different display options, see the latest updates and filter the feed in different ways.

Step 5: Notifications

Notifications keep you updated on everything that's going on in the world of your Facebook network. You'll be informed when anyone likes or comments on any of your posts, and when people reply to posts you've previously commented on. When you view your notifications, new notifications appear shaded. You can scroll down to see older ones.

Step 6: Sharing Via Facebook

As mentioned previously, you don't need to open the Facebook app to use Facebook. Anything you write, find on the internet or photograph can be posted to Facebook instantly. Just tap the usual share button and scroll through the list of sharing options until you see the Facebook icon, then tap it. It really couldn't be any simpler!

iPad Air

Communication Apps

Communication is a huge part of what the iPad is all about and there are apps that can help you do everything from video chatting with friends to finding the perfect date. Here are a few examples.

Find My Friends

Price: Free
Developed By: Apple
In-app Purchases: No

Okay, so knowing where everyone you know is at any time may seem a little controlling, but it actually has its benefits, and using Find My Friends makes it totally possible. Install the app on two iOS devices, accept an invite to follow each other and track away. Just don't do it with people you don't know – that's stalking and you could get in trouble!

Dating DNA

Price: Free
Developed By: Dating DNA Inc
In-app Purchases: Yes

Dating DNA aims to fix people up with the perfect date by matching people more deeply than other similar websites. You have to fill in an extensive questionnaire to get started, giving Dating DNA enough information to match you up with someone with whom you should be compatible. The perfect companion for anyone looking for the perfect companion.

Tapatalk Pro

Price: £2.49
Developed By: Quoord Systems
In-app Purchases: No

If you read a lot of forums it can be tricky to keep track of new posts and threads. Tapatalk takes all the complication out of it, enabling you to access any forum you subscribe to through its own simple interface. You can see at a glance all your new threads and old threads with new posts. If you use forums regularly then you need Tapatalk.

We Heart It

Price: Free
Developed By: We Heart It
In-app Purchases: No

If you love beautiful, inspirational and amazing images then I Heart It is the app for you. It's a community of people sharing their favourite pictures from around the web and also their own photographic work. You can follow people, get recommendations and of course Heart your own favourite images for others. Share in the beauty of art and photography with this great app.

Blendr

Price: Free
Developed By: Blendr
In-app Purchases: No

Blendr is one of the best dating apps around. You can set up a profile, add images and filter the characteristics of the sort of people you want to meet. It comes with a robust messaging system built-in that makes it easy to chat with potential dates, which helps to take the uncertainty out of online dating. Highly recommended for getting to know people online.

Pinterest

Price: Free
Developed By: Pinterest Inc
In-app Purchases: No

In essence, Pinterest is a photo sharing app, but it comes with an angle that makes it a little more interesting. By design it's meant to be a virtual pinboard where you can add images of things that inspire you or that you're working towards, for example, the car of your dreams or perhaps an exotic holiday. Just add them to Pinterest and spur yourself on to make things happen.

LinkedIn

Price: Free
Developed By: LinkedIn Corporation
In-app Purchases: Yes

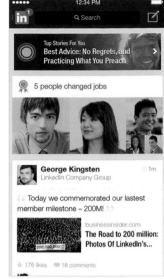

Social networks make the world go round. We keep in touch with most of our friends using Facebook and we get a large portion of our world view from Twitter. It's not all about just being sociable and sharing family snaps though. The professional social network is LinkedIn. If you're a professional in any industry and you're not on it then you really need to be. It enables recruiters and potential clients to find you and see what you're all about.

As you'd expect, the official LinkedIn app distils the website down into a very neat and functional form while still giving you access to all the important elements and features you need. The interface is clear and intuitive so navigation is a breeze.

In the fast moving world of modern business, being in the right place at the right time can often mean the difference between success and failure. Having the facility to stay current with LinkedIn is a big advantage and the app makes it very easy to do so.

This is a very solid, well structured and professional app, but would you expect anything else from LinkedIn? Of course not!

Seesmic

Price: Free
Developed By: Seemsic Inc
In-app Purchases: Yes

Now that Facebook and Twitter are integrated with iOS 6, you might feel you don't need another app to manage your accounts. On the other hand, if you don't think much of the official apps for either social network, Seesmic might be just what you're after. It lets you manage multiple Twitter and Facebook accounts and keeps everything neat and tidy so you can always see what's going on. You can use all of the features you'd usually be able to access through the Facebook or Twitter apps and you'll get pop-up notifications when anyone tries to get in touch with you.

AIM (Free Edition)

Price: Free
Developed By: AOL Inc
In-app Purchases: No

Okay, so maybe you have SMS, Mail, Twitter, Facebook and all manner of other communication apps, but bar iMessage which is obviously limited to iOS-to-iOS messages only, can you instant message without it costing money? With AIM, you can. It's effectively the AOL equivalent of Microsoft's Windows Messenger (which there's also an app for, so you might want to get that too if you already have an extensive network of contacts on your desktop computer), except you can set AIM up to connect with both Google Chat and Facebook Chat as well as using the AIM network.

FlipBoard

Price: Free
Developed By: FlipBoard Inc
In-app Purchases: No

Have you ever thought how great it would be if there was a magazine designed and written especially for you, full of all the things that you're interested in, no matter how obscure or eclectic they may be? Well FlipBoard is that magazine! Add in your interests and this brilliant app goes out into the internet and gathers together everything it can find. The best part is the presentation. Everything is displayed in the style of a digital magazine and not only does it look really cool, but it's really easy to use as well!

iPad Air

165

Communication Apps (continued)

Talkatone

Price: Free
Developed By: TalkMe.IM Inc
In-app Purchases: Yes

Unlike the more popular and well-known Skype, Talkatone is unique in that it doesn't require both ends of a conversation to have the software installed. That means that you can use your iPad as a phone to call pretty much anyone, although the fairly hefty subscription fees charged do make it a bit less enjoyable and practical to use.

Zoosk

Price: Free
Developed By: Zoosk Inc
In-app Purchases: Yes

Ah, Internet dating: isn't it great? It's also the future of relationships (trust us, we've checked on that), so if you're looking for love through your iPad, look no further than Zoosk. The app is an extension of the website and can be used to send messages, check out singles and even find a partner. You have to be a member of Zoosk to use it, of course, but that's the price of love.

WordPress

Price: Free
Developed By: Automattic
In-app Purchases: No

Anyone who's anyone these days has their own website, and most people go for WordPress because it's so easy to use. This app also makes WordPress portable, since it allows you to edit and manage your WordPress website from the comfort of your iPad – handy if you're out and have a flash of inspiration for a new blog post!

TOTALe Course HD

Price: Free
Developed By: Rosetta Stone
In-app Purchases: No

Okay, so the fact you have to own a full version of Rosetta Stone for your computer and a paid-up subscription for this to work is a fairly large catch, but being able to take your language learning course on the road is still incredibly useful if you're heading to foreign lands and want to brush up on your verbiage in transit. It works for all Rosetta Stone languages too, no matter which one you're learning!

Tumblr

Price: Free
Developed By: Tumblr
In-app Purchases: No

Tumblr is a great website and app that enables you to share pretty much anything you like, although it's mostly about images. You can add tags and the like and browse other people's Tumblr pages to see what interests them. It's packed with all sorts of content and if you regularly find yourself on the website then you should definitely download the app.

Yahoo! Messenger

Price: Free
Developed By: Yahoo
In-app Purchases: No

Yahoo Messenger is, obviously, the app version of the excellent Yahoo chat client for PC and Mac. Naturally you need a Yahoo! account to use it but anyone who's used Yahoo! Messenger before will know how good it is. You can text chat, voice chat, video chat, transfer files and more. If you haven't tried it before, now would be a good time to check it out.

Skype

Price: Free
Developed By: Skype
In-app Purchases: Yes

VOIP, or Voice Over Internet Protocol, is a system by which audio and video signals can be transmitted over the Internet, bypassing telephone lines and cell phone signals. It allows free phone and video calls to be made to anyone in the world who has an Internet connection, which is immensely useful if you're trying to keep in touch with loved ones while travelling in other countries.

The big name in VOIP is of course Skype. You've probably used Skype on your desktop computer to video chat with other users; well you can do the same from your iPad with the free official Skype app.

Using Skype you can chat with anyone else who also has Skype, whether they're using an Android device, PC, Mac, smartphone or a tablet. You can chat with video or just with voice, send instant messages, transfer photos, documents or other files, and much more besides.

Skype is such an incredibly useful and powerful app that you'd need a pretty good reason not to have it. If you can't think of one then download it right away because this is the way the world communicates these days. Don't get left behind!

WhatsApp Messenger

Price: Free
Developed By: WhatsApp Inc.
In-app Purchases: No

You may get unlimited free text messages at home, but if you've ever tried to keep in touch with someone in another country using text messaging, you'll know that it can quickly become very expensive. The best alternative is WhatsApp Messenger, a terrific free app created by two veterans of Yahoo! and currently used by over 200 million people. You can send and receive text messages using your normal mobile phone number, but without any hidden costs or international charges. The service is free for the first year, and 69p a year after that.

Gmail

Price: Free
Developed By: Google Inc.
In-app Purchases: No

Google's Gmail is far more than just a web email service; it's the backbone of a network of integrated services that can synchronise your email, contacts, calendar and social networking between multiple devices, as well as your desktop computer. The official free Gmail app for iPad lets you get your email instantly via push notifications; you can read and respond to your conversations online and offline, search and find any email, manage multiple accounts, view and save attachments and set up label notifications. Top stuff.

Status Shuffle for Facebook

Price: £0.69
Developed By: Social Graph Studios
In-app Purchases: No

Anyone who likes to get involved in the world of Facebook knows that likes and comments are what it's all about. What's the point in posting something if no-one responds, right? Status Shuffle contains tons of status update messages that you can post to Facebook straight from the app. All you have to do is choose a category and select a status message that you like. The choices range from funny to thought-provoking but they're all tried and tested when it comes to generating likes and responses. That's why this app is so popular.

iPad Air

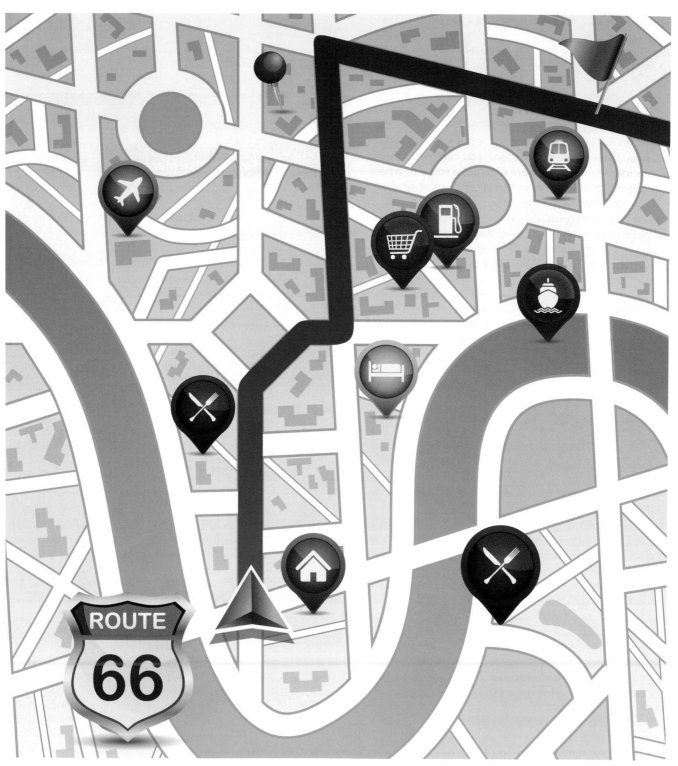

Your iPad Air And
Navigation

Thanks to GPS technology, if you've got your iPad with you (and you have a data connection), you can pretty much always identify where you are and plot a route to where you need to go. If you haven't used any sort of sat-nav or mapping software before, then it all might seem a bit confusing at first, but don't worry – we'll take you through the Maps app in simple, easy-to-follow steps and you'll find yourself getting familiar with it in no time! We also talk you through Find My iPhone. This essential app enables you to locate your iPad (or any other iOS device) through GPS if you lose it. It also gives you the option to lock and delete the contents of your iPad remotely. That way, if it's stolen, you don't have to worry about a stranger gaining access to your contacts, emails and other information. To finish up, we look at some of the top third party navigation apps available in the App Store. If you're the sort of person who likes to get out and about then you may find some of them very useful indeed.

"If you haven't used any sort of sat-nav or mapping software before, then it all might seem a bit confusing at first"

170 How To Use Maps

- On The Map
- Searching For Addresses
- Searching For Landmarks
- Searching For Services
- Further Location Information
- Go 3D
- Zooming In On A Location
- Traffic Overlays
- Hybrid Map Views
- Calculating Routes
- Finding Alternative Routes
- Maps As A Sat-Nav

173 How To Use Find My iPhone

- The App
- Setting Up With iCloud
- Locate Your Phone
- Find My iPhone On A Computer

174 Navigation Apps

- OS MapFinder
- TomTom U.K. & Ireland
- CycleMaps
- Recce – New York
- Commander Compass Lite
- Plane Finder
- Google Maps
- London Tube Map
- Find My Car For iPad
- Spyglass

iPad Air

How To Use... Maps

Provided that you've enabled Location Services and have a network connection in your settings, the Maps app will be able to tell you exactly where you are and how to get where you're going.

Step 1: On The Map

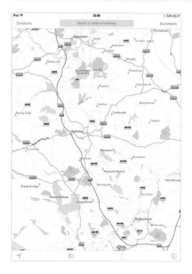

The Maps app, which uses GPS technology to find your location, is already installed on your iPad, so there's no need to go to the trouble of downloading it. You'll need a 3G/4G or Wi-Fi connection to make the most of it though, but it needs to process a lot of data when loading up maps or calculating routes so it will eat up your data allowance, and possibly your battery, as a result.

Step 2: Searching For Addresses

To find a particular location on the map, you can search for it from the top bar by either typing in the address or post code and then tapping Search. You can also find addresses stored in your contacts list via the Bookmarks option in the top right hand corner. To navigate around the map, just drag it with your finger in the direction you would like to explore. It's very easy to scroll around.

Step 3: Searching For Landmarks

The search function isn't restricted to individual street addresses; if you want to find a landmark or tourist attraction such as the Tower of London, type in the name and it should find the location for you. You can even search for wider geographical areas like towns or cities, which will give you a larger map to investigate. Try typing different things in and see what happens.

Step 4: Searching For Services

Maps can also be used to find shops or services near your current location (or another one specified by you). Just type in the search box what you want, for example 'Odeon cinema', and red pins will appear on the map showing local outlets. Tap these to reveal more information about that particular one and you'll easily be able to find your way there using the map.

iTip – LOCATION SERVICES
To get the most out of the Maps app you need to allow your iPhone to use Location Services by enabling the option in Settings.

Step 5: Further Location Information

When you've found a point of interest on the map, there are various things you can do. Touch the panel with the name of the location to show more options and extra information. You can get directions either to or from that point, you can add the location to your contacts list or you can share it by Twitter or email if, for example, you're meeting somebody there. Very handy indeed.

Step 6: Go 3D

In the control bar at the bottom of the maps screen is the 3D button. Pressing this will switch the view from the traditional overhead view to 3D. This allows you to get a better idea of the physical geography of the area at street level, although it's easier to see relative positions in 2D, so tap it again if you want to go back. Useful if you're using the app as a sat-nav.

Step 7: Zooming In On A Location

Drag your finger to move around the map and pinch with two fingers in order to zoom in. If you find the address you want manually, you can add a marker at that point by holding your finger down on it. When a pin appears, tap the panel to check the information or find directions/share/add/ etc. as described in step 5. It's all pretty self-explanatory.

Step 8: Traffic Overlays

Tucked away at the bottom right of the screen are several more useful options, tap the 'i' button to reveal them. A particularly good feature here is the Show Traffic option. When activated, this will show you traffic information for any given location, with green meaning the road is clear, yellow meaning slow, and red meaning very slow. Great for avoiding those delays.

How To Use... Maps (continued)

Step 9: Hybrid Map Views

You can change the appearance of the map to show a satellite photograph instead of the normal map view, or, perhaps of more use, you can display a hybrid of the two with the annotations and features of the traditional map superimposed onto the satellite image. Zooming in allows you to see the lie of the land in some detail and perhaps get a clearer indication of what's around you.

Step 10: Calculating Routes

Getting directions from one location to another is easy. First tap the Directions option to the right of the search field then enter your start and end points in the relevant boxes and tap Route. When you're ready, tap the Start option to engage the sat-nav. Your start point will automatically come up as your current location, but you can change it to anything you like.

Step 11: Finding Alternative Routes

Press Route and Maps will find different ways of getting from a A to B. To see the different options, touch the labels and see which one looks easiest. It will automatically assume you're travelling by car, but if this is not the case, you can tap the icons at the top to get the best routes on foot or by public transport. It makes getting around places a cinch even if you're new to them.

Step 12: Maps As A Sat-Nav

When you've chosen the route you want to take, your iPad can guide you as you travel. Press start and Siri will give you instructions as you go along without your having to touch the phone again until you reach your destination, thus allowing you to keep your hands on the wheel and your eyes on the road. You never need to get lost on your way anywhere again.

How To Use... Find My iPhone

It might be called Find My iPhone, but this app actually enables you to track the location of any iOS device registered to you from a computer or another iOS device.

Step 1: The App

Don't be put off by the fact this app is called Find My iPhone. It enables you to locate your iPad or any iOS device on which you have it set up using GPS. This means you need never worry about where you put your iPad again, or in the event of it being stolen, you can lock it or wipe its contents remotely from another device. Get the app from the App Store.

Step 2: Setting Up With iCloud

You don't need the app to safeguard your iPad. Open Settings and select iCloud and check that your Apple ID is correctly entered in the appropriate box. Then scroll down the list to where is says Find My iPad and flick the switch to the on position. This will enable you to find your iPad using another iOS device, but you'll need the app to locate other devices using your iPad.

Step 3: Locate Your iPad

You need to sign into the app using your Apple ID. When you've done so the app will do its thing and locate your iPad. This may not initially be a particularly useful feature because you ought to know where your iPad is while you're using it, but if your iPad is lost or stolen then obviously it's a great way to find out where it's been left or taken to and could save a lot of tears.

Step 4: Find My iPhone On A Computer

Perhaps more useful is the ability to find your iPad from a computer. You can do so either through the app or in your browser. In a web browser go to www.icloud.com, enter your Apple ID and click Find My iPhone. You will then see a map of your iPad's location with various options of what to do next.

Navigation Apps

The iPad's powerful GPS functionality combined with the many excellent navigation apps available in the App Store make it a great navigational tool for anyone who likes to get out and about.

OS MapFinder

Price: Free
Developed By: Ordnance Survey Limited
In-app Purchases: Yes

The Ordnance Survey is a service that maintains definitive, highly-detailed maps of the UK, and this brilliant app gives you access to them. You can view and download up-to-date OS Landranger (1:50 000) and OS Explorer (1:25 000) maps in high-resolution detail. Additional maps are available as in-app purchases.

TomTom U.K. & Ireland

Price: £39.99
Developed By: Mirage TomTom
In-app Purchases: Yes

TomTom is probably the best-known name in car satellite navigation, used by over 70 million drivers, and this app brings this world-class service to your iPad. It's a very expensive app, and you'll need a subscription to get the full TomTom update service, but what you get is arguably the best in-car sat-nav app on the App Store. It's still cheaper than a standalone sat-nav.

CycleMaps

Price: £1.49
Developed By: SZ Software
In-app Purchases: No

CycleMaps uses the free OpenCycleMaps network to provide a complete listing of bike routes across the UK. The app also includes plenty of options including saving routes and also a selection of routes for when you're outside the UK and looking to take a bit of a ride into the unknown. This is an essential app for all keen cyclists.

Recce – New York

Price: Free
Developed By: mapply
In-app Purchases: No

Recce – New York straddles a difficult line by being both practical and visually stunning. What you get is a completely scalable and rotatable 3D view of the city and it looks amazing. Scrolling around almost feels like you're swooping high above the skyscrapers or you can pinch to zoom in almost to street level. It's worth downloading just to try it.

Commander Compass Lite

Price: Free
Developed By: Pavel Ahafonau
In-app Purchases: No

While it's no substitute for a real navigational compass, a good compass app is a useful standby if you're in the great outdoors, and they don't come much better than this one. It includes waypoint navigation, magnetic compass, gyrocompass, GPS tracker, speedometer, artificial horizon and inclinometer. If you ever need a compass, you need this.

Plane Finder

Price: £2.99
Developed By: pinkfroot limited
In-app Purchases: No

Air travel is stressful enough without having to worry about when your plane will be arriving. This handy app tracks 12,000 flights and planes live at airports all over the world, with a near real-time virtual air traffic radar. Search by flight number, callsign or aircraft registration number. Simply tap on a plane to see all its details. Interesting for all plane buffs.

Google Maps

Price: Free
Developed By: Google, Inc.
In-app Purchases: No

Google Maps has become the go-to navigation tool for the whole world, with comprehensive coverage of 200 countries including both street maps and satellite imagery, and useful information on over 100 million individual places. The design of the app is clean and efficient, letting you easily use the full range of features. Those features include guided turn-by-turn GPS navigation for all forms of transportation including driving, walking, cycling and public transport, with live updated traffic information and incident reports, as well as Google's famous 360-degree Street View function, which covers almost every road in most countries, and now also includes cycle routes and even goes inside public buildings, restaurants, museums and more. If you

have a Google account you can sign in to save your favourite locations and routes, and read user reviews and recommendations about places in your local area. Anything you save in the app is shared across all your devices whenever you log in to your account. The app has been specially designed to use on the iPad, but will also work on iPhone and iPod touch. Download this terrific free app and see exactly what's so darned special about it.

London Tube Map

Price: Free
Developed By: Bappz
In-app Purchases: No

If you've ever been to London you'll have seen the iconic London Tube Map, and you'll know how essential it is if you want to get around in the capital. This excellent free app is far and away the best mobile tube map, and is the most downloaded commuter app in the world, with over two million users. It includes live line status updates, and will work underground because it doesn't require a data connection to run, although you can also use the Virgin Media Wi-Fi service that is available at 120 London Underground stations.

Find My Car For iPad

Price: £0.69
Developed By: Presselite
In-app Purchases: Yes

The Find My iPhone of the motoring world, albeit one that requires a little more effort to function. You simply turn on the app when you park your car to set its location, then reactivate the app when you've forgotten where you put it to see it on a map. You can also take a picture and leave a note to better define where you parked or, if you pay for the augmented reality add-on, see arrows projected on the ground in front of you through your iPad camera. Just make sure you get the right Find My Car app, as there are several with similar titles.

Spyglass

Price: £2.49
Developed By: Pavel Ahafonau
In-app Purchases: No

One for the orienteering types among you, Spyglass takes the basic compass concept and turns it on its head by adding so many features you won't know where to start. From projecting accurate headings on a live camera image and having a sniper-style range finder built in, to providing a sextant, tactical military-style GPS, gyrocompass, inclinometer, maps and even augmented reality navigation highlighting positions of the sun, moon and nearby landmarks, it's every navigation tool in one, with a few more thrown in.

iPad Accessories

There are loads of great and innovative accessories available that can enrich your iPad experience ranging from practical to fun. One thing you'll definitely want to consider is a good protective case.

iPad Smart Case
Price: £39.99

This official product comes in a range of colours. The case also automatically puts your iPad to sleep when it's closed and wakes your device upon opening, making it easy to get straight into whatever it is you want to do.
www.store.apple.com/uk

iBallz Universal Tablet Stand, Case & Harness
Price: £24.95

The iBallz Harness is a truly unique product able fit any sized iPad. Each corner ball has a string through it which can be tightened, so all you have to do is pull the string to make it fit around your device.
www.gearzap.com

Soulo Mic
Price: £49.95

With the Soulo Mic and your iPad you have a cool karaoke experience in the palm of your hand. The mic's quality audio and balanced frequency response brings out the best in your singing and it includes 10 free songs.
www.store.apple.com/uk

Lynktec Truglide Stylus for iPad
Price: £12.99

The Lynktec Stylus provides a smooth, pen-like writing or drawing experience on your iPad. The pen has a soft tip, enabling you to write quickly or move around the screen with comfort and ease.
www.amazon.co.uk

iPad Genuine Leather Cover by Marware

Price: £31.99

This is a fitted leather folio cover that protects your iPad and stands it up for hands-free reading and viewing. All you need to do is detach the two corner tabs closest to the lid and rest the edge of the iPad into one of the two grooves.
wwww.amazon.co.uk

Ted Baker 11" Fabric Flight Bag

Price: £99.95

Designed by Ted Baker, this flight bag is a classy looking design made from leather and tartan. The interior is lined with non-scratch protective padding and there's also an internal document compartment and shoulder strap.
www.storeapple.com/uk

AppleCare Protection Plan for iPad

Price: £69.99

For up to two years from the original purchase date of your iPad, the AppleCare Protection Plan gives you direct, one-stop access to Apple's award-winning telephone technical support. It also includes hardware repair coverage — both parts and labour — on your iPad and its battery.
www.storeapple.com/uk

Just Mobile Highway Pro Dual Charger

Price: £34.95

Turn your drive time into charge time with the Just Mobile Highway Pro Dual Charger. With 2.1 amps, there's plenty of power to give your iPad a quick charge. Not only that but its ultra low-profile design blends nicely into your vehicle's interior. Jeremy Clarkson would no doubt approve.
www.storeapple.com/uk

iPad Air

iPad Air

Uncooked Media Ltd, 3 East Avenue,
Bournemouth, Dorset, BH3 7BW
www.uncookedmedia.com
Telephone 01202 586035

Editor
Miles Guttery

Design
Stephanie Peat

Contributors
Dan Curley, Rod Guttery, Leigh Walsh

Customer Services
08453 306540
customerservice@uncookedmedia.com

Editorial Director
Darren Herridge
wonderdaz@gmail.com

Finance Director
Tim Harris
tim@selectps.com

Printed by
Acorn Web Offset